Hunting The Great White Prawn

by

Ledger De La Bald

Hunting The Great White Prawn

by

Ledger De La Bald

Publisher
Best Books Online
Bronte Media Services

Copyright 2010
First paperback edition published in Great Britain
November 2010 by
Best Books Online
Bronte Media Services

All rights reserved.
No part of this publication may be reproduced, stored in a retrieval system or transmitted in any form or by any means; electronic, mechanical, photocopying, recording or otherwise without the prior permission of the publisher.

Although this story was born on board the *'Prudence'* surrounded by prawn pots, and she was indeed crewed by those with the names Miles and Bald, this is a work of pure fiction. Any similarity to real persons, living or dead is coincidental and not intended by the author.

ISBN: 978-1-906349-15-8

About the Author

Ledger de la Bald was born in 1954 at Brown Bottom, an outlying district of Poole, Dorset. An early love of writing failed to impress his teachers during schooling due to his aversion of writing where, when and what he was supposed to. To the mutual relief of all parties he left school shortly after his fifteenth birthday. After brief forays into a variety of occupations - butcher, boat builder, road sweeper, fruit picker, bicycle mechanic, barman/cellarman to name but a few - he eventually went to work for the Pilot Service, crewing the cutters which conveyed the harbour pilots to and from ships in Poole harbour. This job lasted for 24 years until a suspected case of pogonophobia coupled with spending cuts saw him being made redundant. Alongside of these full time jobs he was writing for magazines, creating and performing poetry in clubs and at festivals as well as writing and acting in the stage production of *'Hunting The Great White Prawn'*.

He now lives in the Pennine village of Haworth, West Yorkshire, with his wife, the artist Karen de la Bald, and is devoting his life to writing and performance poetry. *'Hunting The Great White Prawn'* is his first novel.

Acknowledgements

My thanks are due to those who have helped to nudge this story along into print. These include:
Pete Miles who was there at the beginning, Laurie Fahy who encouraged me to write this book, Maggie O'Hanlon who converted my scrawl of a first draft into a readable form, Barry Ferns for his invaluable suggestions on the final draft. Graham and Margaret Smith who oversaw the whole thing into print, Ant Smith for the photo of the author, Marty Kenney for the front cover design and to the many who enjoyed the stage version and laughed in all the right places.
Last, but not least, thanks to my wife Karen. Without the creative atmosphere in which we live our lives this book would never have been moved beyond the first draft.

Chapter One

Nobody ever visited Holes Bay, at least not the part of Holes Bay where the Visitor now stood. It was not the most attractive part of the harbour, indeed, it would be hard to imagine that it could be part of any harbour so renowned for its outstanding natural beauty. Here in this quiet backwater the mud met the rubble of the long disused power station and the reed beds were strewn with the kind of debris that, after being thrown into the sea, fails to sink and eventually washes ashore in a place where nobody sees any need to tidy up. Here too were the wrecks of old boats, each one having at one time been somebody's pride and joy whether as a vessel of pleasure or as a means of earning a living. Whatever their past they had all fallen into neglect and, once they had reached a point where deterioration was irreversible, had been pulled up on the shore to rust or rot away in their own good time.

The Visitor surveyed this forgotten shore with an irritated frown as he looked around for any sign of habitation. It had not been easy for him to get to this spot, the last half mile being especially hazardous. After following a little used, and much overgrown, path to get to the shore he then found himself by turns clambering over small rocks or through muddy pools to follow its outline. The rocks offered no stability to the footfall and, once his body weight came to bear upon each one, would tilt this way or that causing much discomfort to the ankles. The alternative; walking across the mud at the water's edge, brought its own dangers. In places this mud was quite firm giving an easy passage while in others, without warning, would prove soft and the foot would sink down into it, occasionally as much as six inches. The suction below would then make the foot difficult to extract from the mud without the shoe coming off and being left behind. At these times the Visitor, through a combination of surprise and sudden immobility, had found himself falling over. The hands that automatically went forward to save himself now bore generous traces of this thick black mud, the smell of which was acrid to the point of almost burning the nostrils.

As a consequence of needing to look downwards as he made his way along the shore the Visitor had not had the chance to pay much heed to his surroundings. The most notable incident so far had been when he disturbed a small shore crab whilst negotiating a particularly wet patch of mud. This crustacean had taken the disturbance with little grace and, despite measuring only three and a half inches across its shell, had risen up on its legs and raised its claws in the air: regardless of the Visitor's far greater size the shore crab fully intended to defend its domain. To this end it started an aggressive dance in front of the trespasser, running side-to-side in front of him with the claws snapping threateningly. Its opponent, always a person to avoid confrontation of any kind, undertook a significant detour around the crab.

Having reached the part of the shore that was his destination the Visitor could stop to relax from his arduous journey and take a good look about him. On the opposite side of the bay from where he now stood a number of industrial concerns could be seen, each of them presenting a vista in sharp contrast to his immediate surroundings. The first to catch his eye, due to the high visibility paintwork of the vessels moored around it, was obviously a depot for the Royal National Lifeboat Institute. Lifeboats of all shapes and sizes were very much in evidence and the Visitor, living far from the sea, found himself wondering at all the signs of modern technology clustered around each vessels mast. As a child his grandfather had taken him to visit a maritime museum where he had seen an old photograph of a lifeboat man clad in oilskins, sou'wester and a cork life jacket. This image of the lifeboat service, though he knew it to be outdated, had since that day been fixed very firmly in his mind. Further along this waterfront there were yet more signs of the march of progress into the nautical world. Moored alongside what appeared to the Visitor to be a marina were a number of modern power boats, sleek in design. These craft, being the output of plastics factories rather than built in a traditional boatyard, seemed to the Visitor to be the epitome of soulless mass production. He noted that white appeared to be the popular choice of colour which, when seen as a fleet, reminded him of a row of margarine tubs in a supermarket cold cabinet.

Between that far shore and the one upon which he now stood were a few craft of various types and sizes made fast to mooring buoys. Amongst these one had sunk with only a small section of the foredeck and part of the mast now being visible above the water. It was a forty foot yacht, built of wood and of a design rarely seen these days. In sailing circles such a craft would be referred to as a 'Classic' and, even in its present predicament, it had a fascination that was almost hypnotic. In contrast to the more modern vessels the Visitor found himself wanting to see more of this yacht. He tried to imagine what it would look like inside the cabins, how it would appear under sail. His knowledge of sailing was not through practical experience, as he would be the first to admit, instead it had been gained through the many books that he owned on the subject. He had throughout his life been captivated by the idea of sailing but to actually step aboard a yacht as its Master, resplendent in a peaked cap and Breton shirt, was but a fantasy. He would not, for all his reading, know where to begin. With a sigh he turned his gaze once more to his immediate surroundings and in doing so focused on the reason why he had arrived there.

He had come looking for signs of habitation and he found none. It had seemed that he had been following yet another false lead, this time one that had inflicted many cuts and scrapes on his hands and given him wet mud-strewn feet in his efforts to get there. Looking down at his shoes, glistening damply in the bright sunlight, he was tempted to give way to exasperation at yet another wasted morning. But no, he told himself, you knew this was not going to be easy and you came into this with your eyes open. Even so, another part of his brain reasoned, it really was too bad. He had arrived in the town a week ago, sent by his employers to talk to and make notes about the members of the local Prawning Community. This was his work and it was work that he enjoyed: travelling to different parts of the country, meeting people whose daily lives were far removed from the norm of the city and reporting the details back to his office.

Those employers back at the office indulged in a high level of self-delusion, though no more so than others of their breed. Born with little or no ability to create anything of any use to anyone, they had made their speciality in that arena where large amounts of money was generated out of thin air for, basically, nothing of value whatsoever. These particular overqualified misfits saw themselves at the cutting edge of research. They had, they told each other, been single-handedly responsible for dragging it kicking and screaming into the electronic age - only they possessed the foresight to do this and now they were the acknowledged experts. All of the information that they gathered, on subjects as diverse as astronauts and potato pickers, was indexed, cross-referenced and packaged for marketing purposes. Their client base - which included television companies, film-makers and advertisers - was international and growing: it all worked on the principle that one phrase, one image, one concept, if it caught the public imagination for a season would become extremely lucrative. Something which had the most innocuous of origins in somebody's everyday existence could with the right promotion become emblazoned upon baseball caps and t-shirts across the world. There were, as a consequence, vast profits for everyone concerned: money which a bored and fickle section of society were unable to stop themselves from throwing at such peripheral obsessions. And the raw materials of their product was the information gathered by the Visitor, who was used to an initial reticence on the part of those that he wished to speak to but who could overcame this fairly easily within a couple of days. He had developed 'the knack', the tricks of the trade that would not only make these folk in their close-knit communities drop their wariness of strangers and speak to him but would also have them telling more than he needed to know. For a few days he would become part of their daily lives, eating, drinking and laughing with them and, if need be, working alongside them. By the time he came to leave they would have slight feelings of regret at his going and they would be asking him to be sure to return and visit them again one day. And as he made his farewells he would be taking with him a concise history of these communities and, just as a photographer can capture elusive secrets with a lens, he would have noted the small details which could be exaggerated to fire the public imagination.

But here it was different; it was almost as if the whole town was conspiring to maintain a wall of silence on the subject of the Prawning Fleet. Whoever the Visitor had broached the subject with either responded with a blank look and a shrug of the shoulders or simply turned their back on him and walked away. One old chap, who clearly had the look of a fisherman, had even feigned a puzzled expression and asked what prawns were, he claimed to have never heard of them! Why on earth could they be acting like this? the Visitor had asked himself, it's not as if prawning was an illegal activity. In his research prior to coming to this town he had made himself familiar with the subject and, there could be no mistake in his mind, prawn pots were to be seen stacked up at the Fisherman's Dock. He knew full well that there was a Prawning Fleet here and, he was beginning to suspect, the townsfolk knew that he knew. It was only by chance that he overheard a remark in a cafe the previous day which led him to believe that there was a prawnman living on this shore of Holes Bay but, and this much was clear, there was no habitation to be seen anywhere at this spot. Who indeed would want to live in such desolate surroundings dominated by the overgrown site of a disused power station and an untidy shore line?

Looking around, the Visitor's attention was drawn to the wreck of an old fishing boat nearby. The smell that came from within, although not overpowering, was most unpleasant. Despite this the Visitor found his curiosity was aroused as to its cause. Telling himself that his clothes could not get any dirtier than they were already he walked carefully across the mud and peered into the boat. Although decrepit it was fairly intact, with a cuddy over the bow that seemed to have survived the weather somewhat better than the rest of the structure. On the deck inside this cuddy was a pile of old rags gently steaming in the warmth of the early morning sun and it was from this that the unpleasant aroma emanated. Closer to it was strong enough to make the Visitor wrinkle his nose in disgust and give up his inspection of the boat. But even as he turned away from the wreck a slight movement from amongst the pile of rags arrested his attention. His disgust turned to horror as he realised that this sign of activity proved to be a rat creeping out of its sleeping place and twitching its nostrils in the morning air. In an instant the Visitor feared the worst: the old boat was full of rats, angry rats which were about to attack him. An unreasonable yet deeply ingrained fear, based solely upon a childhood hearing of *The Pied Piper of Hamelin*, gripped him. This fear became panic when, as if on cue, further movements around the pile of rags brought forth more rats. His immediate reaction was to get as far away from the boat as quickly as he could: a difficult task with the soft mud to negotiate. It was due to this necessity to watch each footfall with great concentration that he failed to notice the seagull which had at that very inconvenient moment decided to launch an assault upon him. The first inkling he had of this airborne strike was a sudden loud raucous scream close to his head accompanied by the beating of a large pair of wings. As the bird had approached his position from the direction of the sun it took its target a full eight seconds to realise what was happening to him. This is a very short moment in time but it was long enough to make the Visitor lose his concentration, slip and then find himself sat in the mud.

The bombardment was over as quickly as it had begun. Having made this token gesture the bird flew to a nearby boat and satisfied itself with a few threatening shrieks in the Visitor's direction. The sad and sorry looking recipient of the seagull's fury had no inkling of its cause. This herring gull had decided that it would build a nest nearby and, in preparation, had taken it into its head to warn anybody within its territory that it fully intended to defend that nest. Such subtleties as to why the bird was attacking him were lost on the Visitor. All he was aware of was that he had previously made an incorrect assumption: his clothes could, and had, got dirtier. They were also wet and cold which would make the walk back to his lodgings uncomfortable in the extreme.

Thus the delicate balance: on one hand he was telling himself to give up, this community was determined to thwart him. It felt as though his visit to Holes Bay, during which short time every one of his senses had been assaulted, did not auger well for this project. Not only were the townsfolk making his life difficult for him but, crabs, rats and seagulls, even the small creatures of the town made it clear that they were not best pleased to see him! As these thoughts raced through his mind he knew that, on the other hand, there was his professional pride. This was the overriding factor that would keep him in this town until he had made a breakthrough. With a mixture of anger at his plight and a determination to see this job through, come what may, he rose to his feet and made his way back along the shore. As he retraced the footsteps which had brought him to this place he had lost all concern about his own personal safety. Mud and loose rocks, which had previously served to trick him, he now viewed with a careless contempt, his ill temper carrying him safely through hazards which his earlier caution had not. The shore crab, seeming to realise that this was a man with a mission, prudently allowed him to pass unmolested. Yet even as the Visitor was doggedly making his return journey to the town, back in the cuddy of the wrecked fishing boat the pile of rags sat up, yawned and rubbed its eyes. Rising to his feet and shaking the last of the sleeping rats from within the folds of his clothing, Boathook Bald, crewman on the Prawning Vessel *Prudence,* cheerfully awoke to face the new day.

~~*~~

Just a half a mile away from Holes Bay a rather more salubrious early morning scenario was unfolding. Yet the two were linked, as we shall eventually see.

In the large master bedroom of one of the better houses in the town, warmly cocooned in the finest bed linen ever to grace a four poster bed, a man lay sleeping. Close to the bed hung a uniform that proclaimed its owner to be a seafarer of no little rank in the Merchant Marine. Lying next to him in the bed was a vision of loveliness, the white silk of her nightgown offsetting perfectly the long auburn hair that framed the perfect skin of her beautiful face. They both lay on their backs, their expressions in repose suggesting that the previous evening they had enjoyed an excellent meal accompanied by glasses of the finest wine. Which is exactly what they had done before retiring for the night. In the warmth, safety and comfort of their surroundings they slept deeply and peacefully.

Yet as we look at the man now it is clear that, deep within his subconscious, something is happening to trouble his sleep and making him dream of things totally alien to his present surroundings. For the cause of the frown and the downward turn of the mouth that are the outward signs of this inner disturbance, we have to look at the previous evenings meal. As a first course they had enjoyed a dish that the woman would have identified as Moules Mariniere while the man who, despite his standing in the town, had a rather less pretentious nature, would have called by its local name: a plate of mussels. They had each enjoyed it equally, it was a food to be eaten slowly, a perfect combination of taste and texture to be relished at the time and then forgotten as soon as the next course was brought to the table and laid before them.

It is not always in the nature of mussels to be so easily forgotten however. Once digested they are liable to cause what the woman might refer to as 'excessive wind' whilst the man had a far more graphic term at his disposal. It was this unfortunate side effect of the mussels which, escaping from their bodies, had changed the quality of the air in their bedroom and provoked the man's dream. This involved a pile of rags that, after starting to move around, became clearly identifiable as a person. Stuck in this dream, the man watched in horror as the pile of rags - the same pile of rags from the cuddy of the wrecked fishing boat - grew to monstrous proportions in front of his eyes. Aside from the terror in this dream, another part of the sleeping man's subconscious felt great anger. After all, he told himself, it is bad enough having to have anything to do with Boathook Bald while I am awake, let alone while I am sleeping.

Fortunately the start of this dream coincided with the entry into the room of two more visions of loveliness, their long blonde hair flowing over their white cotton gowns which in turn flowed down their bodies to the floor. On silent perfectly manicured feet they made their way over to the tall windows and folded back the shutters allowing golden sunlight to stream into the room. As the two occupants of the bed stirred from their sleep the two housemaids, for such they were, left the room in order to prepare the waking couples breakfast. Once fully emerged from their slumbers the couple turned to face each other to exchange their customary good morning smiles, but this was the most perfunctory of gestures as the man then turned his eyes to the window. In an instant he had assimilated the wind and weather conditions beyond the panes of glass. Even on days such as this when he would not be putting to sea, and therefore had no real need for the knowledge, his first instinct was to gauge the state of the sea outside of the harbour. Such information ruled his life, but it was the reign of a benefactor rather than that of a tyrant. It was very fine weather the man noted before climbing out of the bed: For Master Miles of the prawning vessel *Prudence* and Admiral of the Prawning Fleet the day was beginning.

The Visitor had arrived back at his temporary abode, a modest bed and breakfast establishment where he cleaned himself up after the mornings mishaps in the mud of Holes Bay. Upon entering the house his landlady - a dear sweet grey haired old lady by the name of Mrs Cousins - had taken one look at his wet and muddy clothes and offered to wash them for him. The Visitor, who had expected to face her anger for entering her home in such a state, felt no little gratitude at this offer and eagerly accepted it. This unexpected kindness was, he decided, a very good omen for his next proposed strategy in tracking down the elusive prawnmen. So far his mode of dress in this town had been one of casual-but-smart. It was his belief that, when approaching such communities, this was the image that projected the right level of friendliness whilst commanding a certain respect. Now he planned to change his approach, going for smart-not-casual, and then pay a visit to the local Vicarage.

From experience he had every reason to believe that this was a good policy, it had served him well in the past in similar circumstances. Local men and women of the cloth knew the folk who formed their congregation intimately. Also, whilst they were generally people who, like himself, were outsiders to the area, they were accepted into the community because of their position. Talking to such a person usually led to an introduction to those who would not otherwise speak to him. To this end, and dressed rather smartly, the Visitor set out through the streets of the town.

The Reverend Michael Grape, Vicar of the parish, shepherd to his flock, comforter of the sick and poor and holy thunderer in the pulpit, had taken up his post some five years previously. His arrival in the town had caused quite a stir among a townsfolk more used to the easy going, devil-may-care attitude of the previous incumbent. Church attendance under that worthy's reign had been a weekly opportunity to meet up, to share gossip, sandwiches and ale, to buy or sell a dog (more often than not dogs were taken into the Church for this very purpose), to play cards and to generally unwind from whatever cares the world had placed upon their shoulders during the previous week. Into this The Reverend Michael Grape had arrived, looked and set his jaw in determination to make changes.

Walking into the Church on the first Sunday of his ministry in the town he roared for silence in a voice that brought forth an immediate response. His physical appearance alone commanded respect: standing at a little under six foot tall with broad shoulders he could, with the removal of his dog-collar, have been mistaken for a bare-knuckle fighter. This illusion was aided by a face which had very clearly spent more of its forty-two years in scowling rather than smiling at the world. His congregation sat as if turned to stone as he then stalked amongst them, much as a hunter might circle its prey waiting for the optimum moment to strike. When finally The Reverend Michael Grape unleashed his storm the petrified flock were thrown into wild confusion. He terrified and then chased hounds out of the church door, he caused grown men to frantically hide playing cards in the manner of errant schoolboys. Brown bottles were rapidly concealed in waistbands while picnics were hurriedly thrown into dark corners or under pews. By the silence that he then maintained while standing among his flock, casting a piercing eye upon each and every one of them in turn, he made it clear that the execution of God's work was a serious and sombre business.

During the course of the following weeks he also made it known that church attendance was a weekly duty which he expected his congregation to observe without fail. Those of his parishioners who had, after this first encounter with the new Vicar, decided that they would stray found no escape. Sunday services could be delayed for up to an hour while he, after noting those who were absent, would set off through the town with a spectral crook across his shoulder to track down the truants and guide them back to the fold.

After a couple of months, when satisfied that he had bent the regular churchgoers to his version of God's will, The Reverend Michael Grape then set out to save the souls of those townsfolk who were unaware of their need for salvation. In this endeavour he met with a variety of excuses:

"Listen here vicar, I'm seventy-five years old. I spent the

first fifty of those at praying. If fifty years of praying ain't enough for him up aloft then nothing I do now ain't going to make no odds is it?"

"I can't spend Sunday in church, it's when I has me hangover. I can't go to church with a hangover and I can't be expected to not have any more hangovers, can I?"

"Mum says we can't go to church 'cos then we'd have to have new clothes and Mum says that's a waste of money 'cos we'd only go and ruin them."

"A'right Vicar, I'll go to church next Sunday if you go and do my bloody nets!"

But God, at least according to The Reverend Michael Grape, did not want to hear excuses. So it was that one by one, without having a clue how it came about other than the fact that the Vicar made it so, each of these straying lambs found their way to church every Sunday morning and evening.

Yet still this scourge of the sinners, intentional or otherwise, was not content. Despite the fact that his church had seen the size of its congregation sharply increase since his arrival in the town he knew that there were folk out there still awaiting the word of the Lord. As he went about his daily business in the parish he saw faces that he never saw when he stood in his pulpit. Furthermore, he did not know where these people went to on a Sunday morning. Asking questions about them among his congregation revealed a general reluctance for anybody to say anything on the subject, demanding answers only brought forth a fearful wall of silence. The Reverend Michael Grape eventually took the view that drastic problems require drastic solutions and asked the choirmaster to join him in the vestry one Sunday after Morning Worship. Once inside the privacy of that room The Reverend Michael Grape lifted the unsuspecting man up against the wall and held his throat in a vice like grip. This approach worked wonderfully and so it was, while exposed to the very real danger of a punch in the mouth, that the choirmaster gave the information which had previously been so elusive. So it came to pass that the Vicar learned of the existence of Paradise, of prawnmen and of sundry other folk to whom church attendance was not a consideration in their weekly lives. Dropping his unfortunate informant to the floor, and pausing only to grab his hat and cloak, The Reverend Michael Grape set off to locate this den of sin and sinners and to put an end to an abominable way of life.

Chapter Two

To the passing stranger, Paradise Street belied its name. This short narrow thoroughfare ran between the bustling High Street at one end and the junction of the Town Quay and Thames Street at the other. For most of its length it was lined on each side by five-storey grain warehouses and the height of these, coupled with the covered walkways that bridged the buildings from the first floor upwards, allowed only a token amount of sunlight to reach street level.

There was an assumption among those who never walked down Paradise Street - and most of the townsfolk would not venture anywhere near it - that the smell wafting from its direction was due to the vast number of pigeons that these buildings attracted or, more precisely, to the droppings that these birds left behind them. However, this thick slippery layer was not the only reason for the gut-wrenching stench. Added to this at any given time there were various rotting corpses, mainly of cats, seagulls and rats. These were strewn among the general litter, fish guts, broken bottles and pools and piles of noisome filth ejected from the bodies of drunks all of which merged into the choking dust emanating from the grain in the warehouses. This dust was generally invisible to the eye, except for when the setting sun was low enough in the sky to send its light into Paradise. Then, for a blessedly few short minutes, it could be seen hanging in the air like a filthy yellow mist. At such times its sickly hue would compliment perfectly the scene of decay and neglect at this spot.

The reluctance of the passing stranger, and of the majority of the townsfolk, to approach this area was seen as a bonus by those inhabitants who did frequent the place. This was largely because in a disused room on the ground floor of one of the warehouses there was a pub of sorts - albeit one with neither a name nor a licence above the door - known to its regular customers simply as Paradise. Owing its existence to the need for the more hedonistic end of the market to have a drinking place of their own, Paradise also provided a safe haven for those whose business lay outside of the law. It was to this place that the working folk of the town made their way when their day's work was done or, in the case of the whores, boarding masters, smugglers and card sharks, when their night's work was just starting.

Inside Paradise the furniture was sparse but solid, built by an old ship's carpenter who, coming to the end of his shore leave and counting his shillings had been more than content to exchange a good days work for a good days drinking. The bar was situated in a corner at the far end of the room, conveniently positioned facing the door. Every person entering would thus immediately fall under the scrutiny of Dave Legg, mine host of the establishment. From this bar he stood sentinel over his small realm and dispensed ale, cider and rum - all of which were produced locally and illegally. The only variation on this bill of fare came either in winter, when each could be served warmed and spiced with ginger, or when some seasoned rum drinkers called for jugs of 'bilgewater'-a peculiar blend of rum, seawater and gunpowder. This beverage was quite unique to the town, though it was a romantically held notion by its aficionados that the recipe dated back to the days of the Caribbean pirates. To the onlooker the drinking of it was seen as a test of manhood rather than for a flavoursome thirst quencher, but to those who partook of the concoction it was viewed as part of their way of life. Bilgewater, they held, was of the town, it was something that set them apart from the rest of the world, it was part of their identity. If a person flinched when offered a pot, or showed any unwillingness to down it, they were shamed in the eyes of their peers: such an offer only being made to those deemed worthy of receiving it. And just as there was a time each year for the start of the cockle season, likewise an annual sprat harvest, so there were occasions upon which the ritualistic sharing of bilgewater had to be undertaken.

Close to the fireplace there always stood a cauldron of stew which simmered constantly and whose origins nobody cared enough to think about. This source of food, the only to be found in Paradise, belonged to everybody and nobody, it was a common pot which was topped up every day with vegetables, whatever fish was plentiful at the time and the dregs of the cider. To partake of this fare it was necessary to wait until your tankard was empty of drink, there being no bowls available, and use this vessel to scoop out the required amount. On a good day there might be a supply of ship's biscuits nearby, liberated from a ship's stores by a visiting crewman and on such an occasion it was felt that the meal was complete. When this was the case the addition of this most simple form of provender altered the manner in which the meal was taken. Without it the diner would partake while holding the cup in both hands, as if trying to emphasise the warming qualities of the broth whilst hiding its meanness. When the fare was augmented with a ship's biscuit there would be a marked improvement in the bearing of the recipient. The cup of broth would be placed proudly upon the table, rather like a battle trophy and its owner would sit on the bench before it, an elbow placed each side and the biscuit held in the fingers of both hands over the steaming fare. As the hard tack was broken, to be dipped into the liquid to soften it, any crumbs would thus be caught in the cup. The meal was then taken slowly, almost delicately, the participant's expression showing a belief that they had been lifted from a soup kitchen and set into *The Ritz* - a notion which would cause them to glance around the room with a superior air. If two or more were dining together they would not spoil their enjoyment with idle chatter. Rather, shared appreciation would be conveyed by a non-stop series of grunts, nods and grins and the time honoured 'thumbs up' gesture passing between them. As this was in stark contrast to the biscuit-less times, when behind the cupped hands would lay squid-like eyes that spoke complaints about life in general, such banquets were an occasion indeed. When the fishing was poor, and the stew started to get on the thin side, a handful of barnacles would be added. It was the generally held view that if the stew had flavour then reason dictated that it must be nourishing.

The wall behind the bar was adorned with a collection of wooden mallets, clubs and belaying pins. All of these items had a practical purpose: they were the weapons that Dave Legg would have no hesitation in using if he thought that any trouble brewing within his walls was getting sufficiently out of hand to threaten his livelihood. On such occasions 'Leggy', as he was generally known, although of no great stature could calm any situation by virtue of his fearsome temper and his ability to wield any two pieces from his makeshift armoury with ambidextrous skill. Such was the reputation that preceded him, Leggy very rarely had to resort to such measures and in any event all of the regulars knew that should Paradise attract too much attention it would get closed down and they would lose it. For this same reason any of the regular patrons who woke in the morning carrying evidence of Dave Legg's discipline upon their body would bear no grudge, rather he or she would make a shamefaced visit to Paradise to offer apologies for whatever they had done. Leggy would always accept the apology without a word of reproach for the situation that necessitated it, there being a general understanding that strong drink had a mind of its own which, every so often, required a special discipline to curtail it. To its recipients this casual violence was no more, and in a lot of cases considerably less, than that which was found in their daily working lives. In one form or another the regulars in Paradise faced untold dangers, be it from a rope breaking under strain decapitating any that stood too close, or from a punter whose smile hid a murderous intent. To Paradise they would go to forget these dangers and Leggy would only step in when somebody needed reminding that a certain protocol had to be observed. Screwed onto the wall above the bar was the only attempt at decoration in the place. It was a length of wood into which were carved the words "*Eat, Drink and be Merry*". It was perhaps unfortunate that the close proximity of the weaponry to this sign gave it the appearance of being a thinly veiled threat rather than a cheerful invitation.

The rest of the room was furnished with three long wooden tables, each with bench seats on either side. Into these tables, which the carpenter had built in situ and which would have been impossible to remove without dismantling either the tables or the doorway, the initials of generations of drinkers and a number of pictures were deeply carved. These pictures fell into two categories. The first and the most skillful consisted of various nautical designs, ranging from simple knot patterns to a very impressive carving of a Man o'War under full sail. The second, and larger, category showed various past and present members of the Town Corporation engaged in lewd, and sometimes impossible, activities with an imaginative array of domestic animals, domestic servants and various other past and present members of the Town Corporation. Among this artwork were scattered the usual stains, burns and candle wax normally associated with any such drinking establishment.

The interior walls of Paradise were of plain bare brick and, although not particularly high, were certainly high enough to allow the periodic impromptu dance sessions that took place upon the tables. The only fixtures adorning these walls were the narrow wooden shelves, fixed at a height just above a man's head, which held rows of candles, the only source of illumination in Paradise – although extra light was afforded when the fire was burning. Underfoot the stone floor was covered with sawdust, sand, straw or nothing, depending on availability and in winter there would be the added luxury of sacking put beneath the tables to stop the worst of the cold from chilling the customer's feet. These sacks, which could be found in plenty around the quayside warehouses, were kept in a pile by the fire and were also used as bedding by those who wanted, or needed, to fall asleep a quiet corner - although 'quiet', with Paradise in full swing, was a relative commodity.

The sacks were also used by the whores who, on occasion, would conduct their business beneath one of the tables. This was not unusual when a visiting sailor or deep-sea fisherman came ashore with a full purse and an urgency in his loins and with little time to empty one fountain before going to the bar to replenish the other. At times like these, once the woman had negotiated a rate with the man and pulled some sacks into position on the floor, her sisters in trade would gather around. By sitting side by side on the table with their feet resting on the floor they would thus form a screen with their skirts. Despite this attempt to provide some privacy, the pair would have to set about their coupling against a background of shouts of ribald encouragement, cat-calls, crude advice on technique and derogatory comments about the woman's cleanliness from the rest of the room. But beneath the table the pair were blind to their surroundings and deaf to those who would debase their lovemaking. For love it was, temporary and the result of a financial transaction it is true, though no less pure for that.

The whores enjoyed their work and took no little pleasure in their ability to satisfy; where other folk may take pride in the finery of their apparel to impress the world, these women had their bodies and viewed their nakedness as a gift of much greater merit than any artificial adornment. And whilst their clients were men simply giving vent to urges that could not be denied, an exchange of money was easy to forget once passion took its grip. At this moment, as with lovers everywhere, the rest of the world would fade into nothingness: conjoined they would look into each others eyes and share the unfathomable secret of life.

Of the three tables, each of which ran almost the entire length of Paradise, there was one on either side of the room and one in the centre. By custom the whores would sit themselves at the table on the right. Here they were not only closest to the fireplace but also furthest from the main throng at the bar and this, as we have seen, was best suited for their business. Among the women there existed a camaraderie and down to earth humour which, given full rein, was highly infectious. Scornful of any puritan suggestion that they should give their business a respectable guise they advertised their wares proudly and, in doing so, they made it clear that they did not feel there was any stigma attached to their work. Nor was there any rivalry between them, trade generally being brisk enough for each to work as much or as little as she wished. Instead they preferred, as they put it, to "watch each other's backs" and in this they knew that most of the local men who were their fellow drinkers in Paradise also offered them some protection. Any stranger in town finding his way into Paradise and showing an interest in the whores would have at least one of the men leaning close to his ear with the advice:- "Mind you look after her, and pay her well." spoken in a tone that left the stranger in no doubt that this was advice he would do well to heed.

Unspoken leader amongst the whores was Granny Lipton, 'Granny' being an affectionate nickname due to her age rather than her family status as she had borne no children. A grey haired woman of some fifty-six summers, she commanded respect on the strength of her family name. The Lipton clan were known as people not to be trifled with: not too many years past they had been in business as boarding masters, those quayside sharks who were both the blessing and the curse of simple sailors everywhere. The boarders were to the merchant fleet what the press gangs had been to the Royal Navy, although the press gangs did adhere to certain rules. Not so the boarding masters, their services were used by the class of ship that had such a bad reputation that no sailor in his right mind would willingly walk across the gangplank to sign on as crew. The Skipper of such a vessel would have no qualms about signing over a hefty percentage of each man's pay for a voyage to the local boarding masters. By using the twin lures of strong drink and dockside whores these vultures would then set out to shanghai a crew. Their victims would soon, beaten insensible, be delivered to the ship and locked below decks until the vessel was well clear of port and by the time they regained their senses they had no choice other than to work at whatever duties that they were assigned to. As they had generally been packed off to sea with only the clothes they stood up in, a further inroad into their pay for the voyage was made by the Skipper supplying them with wet weather gear from his slop chest - at a price inflated beyond reason. Such sailors returning to shore after months, or even years, at sea with little or nothing to show for their back breaking labours would quite often walk willingly into the boarding houses. Here they were able to enjoy a short period of unlimited pleasure, which they had no other means of obtaining, before being sent off to sea once more. It was the regime of a "live today, pay tomorrow" philosophy which was weighted heavily against the humble sailor.

It was Granny Lipton's proud boast that, as a young woman, there was no one else in her family as willing and as successful as she was for the part she played in this work. In her youth she was possessed of a rare beauty with which, deftly used, she could beguile any man. If she had been born into a higher class of society she would have secured, at the very least, a Duke in matrimony. To the possibility of high rank she was, however, blissfully ignorant. Instead she would quite eagerly use her charms to secure the attentions of sailors desperate for the touch of gentle flesh. Once entrapped with promises spoken by her lips and implied by her eyes the man's unwitting visit to the boarding house was a foregone conclusion. Within those walls the sensual spell would be abruptly broken, in its place the systematic brutality deemed necessary for the trade of boarder would take over. This violence would, however, be no more than was required to render the man pliant to his assailants wishes, for no Captain wished to pay for a less than able seaman. The young Lipton girl would regard the poor sailor's downfall with a detached air before asking, simply: "How many more do we need tonight?" Receiving an answer she would once again take to the streets and alehouses in search of her prey.

The sailors numbered among the local men knew full well the game that was being played and could not generally be counted alongside the unwary. Instead they watched the young whore's masquerades with the joy of avid spectators, taking great delight in the gullibility of those within her sights and making fatalistic predictions about their immediate future. As these local men knew which ships were due in port, and which of these would require a crew by means fair or foul, they were well placed to speculate. The Captains who would arrive and seek the services provided by the Liptons were known to them all. Some of these Captains paid poorly, others allowed their ships to become close to unseaworthy for the want of a routine dry-docking. A few were known for their insistence that young sailors should perform a dual role on board ship: as well as duties more usual to the hands manning a ship they would also be expected to satisfy the Captain's carnal desires. The local men took a professional pride in being able to accurately guess which of the young Lipton woman's victims would end up on any given ship. When her gaze was directed toward an athletic youth, keen but still naïve, there would be much nudging and knowing looks exchanged among these spectators. On occasions these looks would be accompanied by one of the men emphasising the youth's fate by the pulling of an agonised expression whilst clutching at his buttocks and jumping up and down on the spot. Such tom-foolery was always well received by his companions.

Though watching this mock paramour at her work gave

much amusement to the local sailors, they also had an underlying reason to study her progress. Although the Liptons would usually only take unsuspecting visiting sailors there was always the danger that these would not be enough to meet the demand. It was not entirely unknown for a local man making his way drunkenly home to be waylaid by the boarders to make up a shortfall. Therefore, the more successes chalked up by the whore meant greater safety to the local men.

From time to time old sailors would seek out Granny Lipton when they were in port, to share a few jars and to chide her light-heartedly for some of the terrible voyages she had sent them on in the past. These old salts bore no grudge for the treatment they had suffered: they had always been aware of the activities of the boarding masters in various ports and they accepted it as part of their way of life. When ashore it became almost a game to outwit the boarders and when the sailor lost the game, after giving a few perfunctory curses, he would shrug his shoulders and get on with his work.

In her later years, Granny Lipton's particular trick, which she only played upon visiting sailors, was to take a man into Paradise and get him to buy her drinks all evening while encouraging him to drink a similar amount. By surreptitiously passing her tots of liquor to her friends and by topping up the man's glass from her own she would, quite literally, drink him under the table where he would collapse in a drunken heap. There she would leave him sleeping, only joining him at the end of the evening with a good supply of sacks to keep them both warm. When they awoke in the morning she would claim to the hapless fellow that he had made full use of her services the night before. She would demand, and get, full payment in return. After the man had paid up and gone on his way Granny Lipton would hold his money aloft in triumph, crying: 'Look at that, and he didn't get as much as a sniff!'

The table on the left was always the fullest at any time of day or night. At this table would sit a collection of fisherman, seafarers, both deep sea and shore based, dockers, idlers and loafers, ne'er-do-wells, sots and dandies, fishwives, housewives, mistresses, anyone, in fact, who lived and worked in the town and who felt uncomfortable, or unwelcome, in the more conventional public houses nearby. Folk who sat at this table (folk that Dave Legg, without a trace of irony, would refer to as his 'Rogue's Gallery') would always try to secure a seat on the bench that backed onto the wall. There were two reasons for this: there was not only the advantage of having the wall behind that served as a backrest but also, and more importantly, it was wise to sit facing any trouble that might flare up. In Paradise this could happen at any given moment and when it did so it tended to be unforeseen, sudden and violent. Between the time that a fight started and the point that Leggy waded in to put a stop to it, both arms and legs fully employed, the unwary could find themselves caught up in the melee with painful results. For this reason, those arriving too late in the day to get to one of the preferred seats would position themselves on the other bench, either astride it or, if space did not allow this, with their backs to the table. Any discomfort this caused to the spine was reckoned a small price to pay for personal safety.

The central table bore the nickname 'Devil's Island', and if that cloven hoofed scourge of the pious folk ever found his dark place lacking in demons he would find, sat at this table, plenty of candidates to address the deficiency. Here were the regulars who feared nobody or whose mental state grouped them into the class of person known locally as 'head-bangers'. Some of these, and Bish Salisbury was a good example, carried with them an air of unpredictable violence wherever they went and could never be trusted, even by their closest friends. Standing at six foot two with an uncontrollable shock of dark curls upon his head Bish was known to be at his most dangerous when he smiled. Whilst this eye twinkling, joyous, expression would light up a room if spread across a countenance of a more stable member of the community, in this instance it served as a warning: the only thing that made Bish Salisbury smile was the thought of hitting somebody. For those innocents who found themselves the target of Bish's random aggression, the first line of defence was always to plead their case – in terrified tones; "Wassup Bish? I aint done nothin'." Though, knowing such words were futile in stemming an attack, they would be uttered merely as a delaying tactic whilst seeking a route for flight, escape from whatever was causing Bish's jollity being the only means of saving oneself from its inevitable painful outcome.

Equally to be avoided were characters such as Pete Emery who were harmless enough in everyday life but believed themselves to be lions when the drink took their wits away. At one time the Master of a prawning vessel, Pete Emery had lost his boat, and therefore his livelihood, through his own actions. Sober the man could reflect upon and accept his foolishness but this was not so when he was drunk; at these times he bore a grudge against the world and all those in it. His position on the central table reflected the friendless station of his existence: as a Master he had been disliked by the crews and their hostility toward him had not been softened by the downturn in his fortunes. When he walked into Paradise of an evening his arrival elicited no greetings from the company and nor did he expect to made welcome.

Instead he would sit alone with his cider, staring at nothing in particular at some point in the middle distance, and drink himself into dissatisfaction.

As a rule the alcohol would only affect his facial muscles, the resentment festering in his thoughts being brought to life via scowls and sneers directed at the cider pot in his hands until, eventually, some inner voice would convince him that he had drunk enough. He would then stand and shuffle toward the door, his exit engendering the same level of interest as that shown at his arrival. But on other occasions the bitterness within would erupt with volcanic fury and this small man would leap to his feet declaring war upon every person who happened to be in range of his vision. The flailing fists which he then whirled around like the sails of a demented windmill could only cause real harm by chance, Pete Emery not being one possessing the necessary skills to fight effectively. But this was a chance that few were willing to take and floor space was given until, through drunkenness or weariness, he fell to the ground. Thus rendered less of a danger, the opportunity to rapidly evict him from the premises would be seized before he had time to rise once more.

Set amongst the head-bangers were the likes of the Lipton boys who used their physical strength as a means of earning a living – whether fully legal or not making little difference to them. Outside of work they lived on their family reputation and would not bow down to anyone. They carried anger in their eyes from waking till sleeping and had ready fists to bring it to life, to the point that outsiders dare not even mention the family name in case one of its members perceived a slight. A slight which would bring immediate retribution. They were the unspoken wardens of the middle table, none could sit there without their grudging approval.

Onto this Devil's Island would sometimes wander an unsuspecting visiting sailor, one who had heard of the existence of Paradise without being made aware of the protocol to be observed within. When this happened he would be made aware that; "You are sitting in somebody's seat mate" and this was usually enough to make him realise that he had not shown good manners and he would move to the table on the left. Here he would be made most welcome - for visiting sailors always had a tale or two to tell and for those who inhabited this small realm it was their only glimpse of the world beyond its shores. If, through stupidity or stubbornness, he refused to move from the middle table he would be unceremoniously ejected from the premises. Those guilty of the latter would be dealt with swiftly and roughly: justice in the hands of those dispensing it not being of the kind that wasted words in discussion on the matter. The fools were treated more kindly though no less firmly and for these offenders there was the humiliation of discovering that they were not even worth raising a fist to on their way out of the door.

The middle table did, however, welcome musicians to sit amongst them. For those who could strike up a tune, whether on fiddle, guitar, squeeze-box or vocal cords, an evening's free drinking was guaranteed. When Paradise was hosting one of its impromptu music sessions it took on a different atmosphere, everyone within being transported away from their everyday cares. Folk who had been ready to pick a quarrel over something or nothing would, of an instant, discover a new-found inner contentment. Furrowed brows gave way to laughter lines while lips more used to curses would relax and mouth the words to the songs. Hands usually carried balled into fists would open, their violence metamorphosed into enthusiastic applause. As the tempo of the music started to gather pace the listener's feet would then join in with the rest of the body. At one extreme this would involve simple foot tapping whilst at the other it could break into a more vigorous activity. The participants liked to refer to this as dancing, though an onlooker, ignorant of its cause, may not recognise it as such. Indeed, the sight at times could be quite alarming and even threatening as limbs were forced into contortions beyond their natural limits. At these times the essence of Paradise became a tangible entity: keeping itself hidden (although the rest of the townsfolk would have to be accomplished liars to claim no knowledge of its existence) while glorying in its own illegality and defying anyone to walk in and stop its customers from doing exactly as they wished.

Paradise may have acquired its name through an accident of location and in a spirit of ironic humour but for its customers there were moments when Paradise appeared to be within their grasp. Just as it bred its own violence and dealt with it, so it created its own pleasures and shared them liberally amongst the company within its walls.

Chapter Three

Needless to say, The Reverend Michael Grape's mission to Paradise could be summed up in one word: failure. Two hours after setting out with such high resolve it was a very dejected man who sat in the great armchair of his Vicarage. The fire was burning brightly in the grate before him but he felt no warmth, he just felt sick, sorry and utterly defeated. He had never known failure before and on that count it hit him doubly hard. He was also struggling with his conscience which was telling him that he may well have committed a sin. Finding Paradise from the choirmasters choked directions had been easy. Getting into the place had not been so easy but he had done it. Once inside his great voice called for silence – but silence did not come. Again and again he repeated his call but to no effect. Confronting the people within individually, with the wrath of God to back him up, brought the same response in every instance - he was completely ignored. All around him the drinking, fornication, fighting, singing, shouting and swearing continued unabated. Eventually he had taken off his hat and cloak to draw attention to his vestments which, at least, had held some curiosity to one pair of eyes in the room. Would that they had not, the Vicar now thought bitterly. One of the whores had walked up to him, raised her skirt to show that she did not allow underclothes to get in the way of her trade and announced that she had never in her life had intercourse with a man of the cloth. She further made it clear that, this being the case, she was more than willing to satisfy the Vicar's every desire for no financial return. In the course of extending this invitation the woman had used the very same phrases that she would have used when addressing a common sailor, uttering crudities which the Vicar had found most distressing. As if this was not bad enough, she then turned and bent over. Lifting the back hem of her skirt high, she emphasised that there was more than one point of entry and that the Vicar could take his choice. So dumbfounded at this was The Reverend Michael Grape that at this instant he failed to avert his eyes from this wanton pubic display, so committing what he now believed to be his sin. Suddenly brought to his senses by the awareness that those in the immediate vicinity were laughing uproariously at the whore's actions, the Vicar started believing that he had fallen into hell itself and had beaten a hasty retreat out into the fresh air. Momentarily forgetting his mission, he was more concerned with seeking reassurance that the world he knew still existed and this caused him to return to the Vicarage at a pace little short of running. Once he had closed the front door of this, his only sanctuary, he discovered that he still could not escape Paradise. Every last detail of his visit to the place seemed to be etched into his mind and, when he did try to replace these thoughts with something less sordid, he could only torment himself with that one word: failure. Not only did he feel a sense of failure over this visit, he also felt the future failure of knowing that he would never go back there. This hurt him. Eventually, realising that his brooding upon the experience was only serving to cause him anguish, he rose from the armchair and busied himself with preparations for the evening service. But he carried on his duties that day with a heavy heart and with such an air of distraction that, dressing to go to his church for Evensong, he totally failed to check inside his hat. Had he done so he would have noticed that during the time it was not upon his head whilst inside Paradise it had been much used as a spittoon.

In the ensuing weeks his inability to make any headway into this part of his parish started to affect his everyday life. He continually asked the Lord for a sign, something tangible to show him why this Dante's inferno existed on his very doorstep. If a sign was given, he failed to see it. After a while he could only visualise Paradise as inherently evil, along with the people who frequented it. They were the servants of Satan. Thinking about this once too often took him a step further: the only word that stuck in his mind from the choirmasters strangled description of Paradise was 'Prawnmen'. In his by now cracked view on the world prawns were also the Devil's creatures.

The following Sunday he preached a sermon that even by his own standards was thunderous. The evil brought into the world by prawns was its subject, with exhortations to his flock to strike this filth from their diet. For three hours solid he stood in the pulpit, strode the aisles of the church or knelt in front of the altar with his arms raised, all the time quoting obscure passages from the scriptures which he felt were God's direct messages to the world telling its people to beware of prawns. By the end of the service he had stretched the credulity of his congregation to the limit: sidelong glances were exchanged, looks that conveyed serious doubts about the Vicar's sanity. The Misses Goodchild clutched at each other's elderly hands in fear and both seemed quite prepared to burst into tears. The more articulate witnesses to the sermon were fully intending to write to the Bishop of the Diocese, questioning the choice in appointing The Reverend Michael Grape to this Parish. The one exception to this startled reaction was the choirmaster who, since his interview in the vestry, was prone to void his bowels and drop into a faint whenever the Vicar raised his voice.

In the years that followed this outburst there was nothing in the conduct of The Reverend Michael Grape to suggest that he was unfit to continue with his ministry in the town. He carried out his duties up to and beyond the letter. It is, however, important to bear in mind that this man's image of the Devil no longer had horns, cloven hoofs and a pointed tail. To him, the sign of evil incarnate upon Earth had now assumed the shape of the humble prawn. The Reverend Michael Grape is the very man whose door the Visitor set out to knock upon when hoping to find a friendly ear in his efforts to find out more about the Prawning Fleet.

~~*~~

Master Miles sat at the breakfast table looking at his morning post and fiddling with his coffee cup. By raising his eyes slightly he was able to steal a glance at the vision of loveliness sitting opposite and to drink in her beauty. As he did so he thought to himself, as he did every morning, that it was a pity that her name was Hilda. This was a slight irritation to him for some reason. His eyes returned to the pile of letters: two bills, three items of junk mail, another of those anonymous letters that said simply 'GET THEE BEHIND ME PRAWNMAN' and a nice fat cheque from one of his customers. As the fat cheque far outweighed the sum of the two bills he was happy with the world, or nearly happy. He still carried in his mind the intrusion into his dream of Boathook Bald, his crewman on the *Prudence*. How dare he? Still, he told himself, today was the day of the hiring, the day when by tradition he could change his crew if he so wished.

The Masters of the vessels that comprised the Prawning Fleet enjoyed the day of their hiring of a crew for the coming season, an event known locally as 'The Stench Fair'. It had not always been such an occasion to look forward to, in fact for many centuries it had been a fairly mundane affair. By tradition it had taken place on the first of May every year and had been known, quite simply, as 'The Stench' - a stench being a colloquialism for any gathering of prawnmen. Upon that day all the Masters in the fleet requiring a crew would make their way down to the Fisherman's Dock. Each of them would be carrying in his pocket a pebble with the name of their vessel written on it, to be placed in a wicker fish basket upon arrival. Already gathered at the Fisherman's Dock would be all of the crewmen who were seeking a seasons work and, as a mark of respect to the Masters, these men would be stood in a spot downwind of where their superiors would congregate. Upon the church clock striking the last chime of noon the Admiral of the Prawning Fleet, by tradition this being the Master who had landed the biggest catch of the previous season, would take up the basket and cast the pebbles in the direction of the assembled crewmen. There would then follow a mad scramble among these hopefuls as they fought to grab one of these prizes, with the amount of violence that they would inflict upon each other to secure such trophy being far greater in years when their number was much higher than that of the pebbles. Those who walked out of this affray with a triumphant look upon their face would read the name written on the little stone. This name, for better or worse, would be their berth for the coming season. They would then locate their respective Masters to discuss the terms and conditions of employment and the simple act of handing back the pebble to the Master signified their acceptance.

But to Master Miles and his peers in the Prawning Fleet The Stench was not within their living memory. Traditions evolve and change. A major alteration to this centuries old way of life was brought about some ninety years previously by the arrival in the town of a direct rail link with London. Suddenly it was possible for local catches of prawns to be transported to the capital overnight and this brought about an attractive increase in the prices that were paid to the Masters. Thus, men who had once lived in the next street to their crewmen, albeit in slightly larger houses, now lived on the other side of town in much bigger homes. Inevitably this new elite decided among themselves that they did not want to get so close to the crewmen on the first of May each year: they wanted their position at The Stench to reflect their new found status.

And so they found a new venue, on the Town Quay. To the Prawning Masters this represented a move away from the somewhat grubby area where their actual work was done to a place which was surrounded by evidence of the towns prosperity. The Town Quay, whilst still very much part of a working port, was starting to be seen as an attractive place for affluent families to take a Sunday stroll. Artists and photographers, also, were targeting this waterfront and their bohemian status served to bridge the gap between those who performed manual tasks and those who did not. This, in its way, created an air of respectability allowing the prawning Masters to feel that they had truly stepped up in the world when they took the lease on part of a quayside building which they now used as their own private club. It was in front of this building where, now renamed 'The Stench Fair', their annual hiring took place.

In deference to tradition, various aspects of the original

Stench were incorporated into the fair. May the first was kept as its date as this was a convenient time of year for it and the pebbles were also still used as it was felt that too much change would bring bad luck to the fleet. The most noticeable difference to the days proceedings was in the form of a large marquee set up upon the quay. Within and around this ostentatious blaze of white canvas the Masters would meet a good two hours before mid-day to parade their wealth. Tables would have been set up inside the marquee, tables that held a goodly array of fine food and drink for their consumption with overindulgence in this fare being obligatory for the Prawning Masters and their invited guests. This latter group tended to be business associates of the Masters, fishing boat skippers who were also doing rather well through the increased trade and perhaps one or two of the more compliant members of the Town Corporation. Pride of place in this marquee was given to a clean fish basket filled with highly polished pebbles - though the custom of marking these with a vessels name had by now fallen into disuse.

Across a short stretch of water, on a quay facing this display of wealth, stood the crewmen who were looking for work. They would have arrived at their appointed place several hours before the rest of the town had been awake, hoping to secure a position close to the edge of this quay. Talk amongst these men at this time would be almost non-existent, each of them taken up with their own private fears for the outcome of this day: to have a year's work or to not. Once the Masters began arriving on the quay opposite the eyes of the crewmen would follow their proceedings anxiously, for although all of the Prawning Masters attended the fair not all of them needed to seek a crew. Some of the Masters would have decided to keep their crewmen from the previous season and these men would be notified of this just before mid-day via a messenger sent over from the marquee. For the crewmen who were not so fortunate the tension heightened greatly as the minutes passed before the church clock struck twelve. Having seen which Masters were keeping their crew they would know what number of berths would be available for the coming year and nowadays it was always a lesser number than that of their own gathering.

As the first stroke of noon echoed around the town the scene on each side of the quays would suddenly change. On the crewmens' side there would be much jostling and, in lean years, even fighting to gain a place close to the quay edge. Men who had spent the morning slouching with their hands in their pockets were suddenly stood bolt upright and using their arms and shoulders to give their bodies extra width. Those who had moved too close to the waterfront could well find a boot making contact with their buttocks: being thus suddenly pitched over the edge they would lose vital minutes as they fought to regain dry land. It was unashamedly every man for himself in this battle to secure a berth in the Prawning Fleet. Over on the Town Quay, meanwhile, the basket of pebbles would be ceremoniously carried out of the marquee and placed a few feet back from the water's edge. Those among the Masters who required crew would stand around this basket whilst the others gathered around to watch the fun.

Upon the twelfth stroke the Masters gathered around the basket would each take a catapult from his pocket and proceed to fire pebbles in the direction of the assembled crewmen. The rule was simple: if you got hit, you got work. Whilst this rule was simple getting hit was not always so straightforward, for with two hours of steady drinking behind them the Masters tended to send more pebbles astray than in the right direction. Those shots that did, by some freak accident, head towards their intended target were sometimes aimed too high. It was not unusual for the crewmen to leap into the air when this happened, hoping to make contact with the missile. Much excitement would be generated by a man who received a clean 'hit': it was a generally held view that a Master who could show such ability whilst drunk must have great navigational skills, a man who it would be safe to sail with. Standing to one side of the Masters would be an appointed adjudicator whose job it was to keep a record of which crewman had secured a berth, and with which Master. Once he signalled that all the crewing requirements of the Prawning Fleet had been met, the Masters would return to the marquee to continue the days feasting and drinking with renewed vigour. The adjudicator, meanwhile, would make his way over to the quay where the successful crewmen were waiting to be allocated their berths for the coming year.

Still sitting at the kitchen table, Master Miles let his mind wander to thoughts of the coming season. Although he would be selecting his new crewman this very day, the prawning season did not start for another three months. Between the first of May and the first of August there would indeed be plenty of prawns out in the bay but, as it was their spawning time, no Master would go out to set his pots. To not allow the prawns their breeding space would spoil their livelihood for many years to come. For this same reason each Master would keep an eye on his catch at the start of the season and, as the pots were emptied into the baskets, any prawn seen to be carrying eggs would be carefully picked out and returned to the sea. Between today and the beginning of August the crewman would be set to work on maintenance of the boat, repairing and tarring the pots, cockling, painting the Master's house, cleaning his boots, walking his dog - in fact anything the Master wished to do with him. Once he had hit the man with a pebble the crewman was effectively the Master's property for a period of twelve months, to be worked as hard as possible and to be paid as and when the Master allowed such a consideration to enter his mind. Such was the tradition of the Prawning Fleet and, even if he wanted to, who was he to change it? Life, the Admiral reflected, was good to him - but this was no more than he expected as one born into a long line of Masters in the Prawning Fleet. Their high standing was something which they could, and did, take for granted – without their guiding hand a whole way of life in the town would crumble away to nothing. Had Master Miles known that, at that very moment, a letter was being posted, the contents of which could shake the very foundation of this small community, he would not have allowed himself the smile of great satisfaction which spread across his face. In blissful ignorance of this letter he shared this smile with one of the housemaids as she wafted across to the kitchen table to refill his coffee cup. As she leaned forward to carry out this task he noted her great beauty, while at the same time thinking it a great pity that she too had been named Hilda.

Suddenly the scene of morning calm was rudely broken by a loud hammering of fists upon the kitchen door. Before any of the occupants of the room could react the handle was turned and the door, being unlocked, swung open. The wild eyed, terrified, bedraggled figure of the Visitor then fell over the threshold into their presence and, on hands and knees, crawled into the farthest corner of the room. He had just come from the Vicarage.

"Help me! Please save me! "he gasped from his position on the flagstones.

"How dare you burst into my home like this," shouted the indignant Master Miles, leaping to his feet "Get out!"

"Please," the Visitor looked up with a desperate expression "I've got money, I'll pay."

"Come and take a chair at my table," said a now genial Master Miles, "Hilda, get the poor chap a cup of coffee."

While the Visitor sat drinking coffee and regaining his composure his host regarded him with a financially critical eye. By studying the cut of the clothing and the quality of the wristwatch he could get a fairly accurate estimation of how much money was available here. He knew who the man was, in fact every Master in the fleet was aware of the Visitor's purpose in the town. In much the same way that they might study a stretch of sea, deciding where to place their pots for maximum profit, they had played this man along knowing that eventually he would pay for the information that he had walked into the town hoping to get for nothing. It was by lucky chance that, following a terrifying encounter with The Reverend Michael Grape, the Visitor had stumbled upon the home of Master Miles. Lucky, that is, for the prawnman. Not only would he profit nicely from his unexpected guest, he would also clean up on the wagering that had taken place around the Fleet, the purse going to the Master who succeeded in landing this particular catch.

Master Miles had only one regret: he had been intending to rid himself of Boathook Bald that day but, as it had to be acknowledged, there was no other crewman in the fleet who could give the visitor the information that he wanted. It had been a matter of pride to successive generations of the Bald family that they had never abandoned the prawning, not even during the years when prawns had been few and far between. Their finely tuned sense of the social order into which they were born gave them an unshakeable belief in the traditions of the Prawning Fleet. Directly above them in this status quo stood their Master, whose word they followed without question: below them there were only the prawns. Mother Nature had decreed that the reason for a crewman's existence was to serve the first by catching the second. To even think of attempting to change their station in life would, to the Balds, be against all natural laws. They proudly laid claim to being the very first family that had served in the fleet as crewmen, on a day they vaguely referred to as 'Way back in 'istory'. This, they believed, gave them the responsibility to ensure that the traditions were observed by all. And whilst it could be said that conventional schooling was something that they preferred to dispense with, their knowledge of the customs and traditions of the Prawning Fleet was second to none. From the cradle to the grave this formed the dogma by which they lived their lives. Furthermore it was a subject upon which, given the opportunity, any member of the Bald family would eagerly share their knowledge. Their world was small and they very rarely looked beyond its sphere: within that world they knew their place and found their security in maintaining it. And it would have to be a crewman who talked to the Visitor: for, as a matter of professional pride, no Master in the Prawning Fleet would take money for something and then do the work himself.

As these thoughts tumbled through the Admiral's mind he kept a very careful eye upon the Visitor. The subject of his scrutiny was completely unaware of his host's interest, he was more intent on sitting hunched over his coffee cup and giving startled glances toward any sudden sound from without the door. The housekeeper was ignored by both of the men as she busied herself with routine dusting and allowing herself the occasional curious look in the Visitor's direction: an observer might note that she was displaying a great need to mother this man. Master Miles, for his part, neither knew nor cared about what had happened to put the man into such a trauma. What was clear is that it would be in the Master's interests to wait for the optimum moment to start talking money. Obviously the Visitor needed time to recover from whatever ordeal he had suffered, but not too much time. He needed to be kept at a disadvantage so he was nearly, but not quite, able to think straight. When the right moment came it was the start of twenty minutes spent in serious negotiation, at the end of which the prawnman's pocket had been swelled by a sum which was double the amount that the Visitor had in mind as the absolute upper limit. On top of this it had been made clear that, during the course of the talking, the crewman would expect his drinks to be supplied - a further expense to the Visitor but, he was assured, it would be well worth it.

"Very fine to do business with you," said the Master, shaking the Visitor by the hand as he stood up to leave.

"You will find my man sat on the bench outside the Town Cellars at nine o'clock tomorrow morning.

Chapter Four

"Red sky at night,
An' prawnin's alright,
Red sky in mornin',
We aint goin' prawnin'".

"That's one o' ours that is," declared Boathook Bald. He looked the Visitor straight in the eye for a few seconds before turning his attention to the glass of rum that had just been placed in his hand.

As the prawnman was thus engaged the Visitor took the opportunity to study the man who, he had been promised, would tell him all that he wished to know about the local Prawning Fleet. The first impression of his informant was encouraging: he certainly had the look of one who spent his life by the sea. In age he could have been a person in his mid-twenties to whom life had been harsh or one in his mid-forties that had been dealt a kind hand. In truth he was thirty-five and liable to appear as either of these, depending on how the world was treating him on any particular day. In dress he looked the very caricature of a fisherman in the rig of smock and waders, these garments complimented by a full beard. But this depiction, favoured by artists and actors alike, rarely portrayed the reality that was to be observed at close quarters: the smock had clearly lived through better days, if not decades, being frayed at all edges and bearing much evidence of repairs and patching. The waders were perished and cracked in places making the Visitor wonder if they were still capable of serving their intended purpose. He was not to know how pleased the prawnman was with this footwear: found only a week before, discarded in a rubbish bin, they were the perfect replacement for his previous pair of waders. These had actual splits around the heels and could be most uncomfortable when wet which, inevitably, they frequently were. Boathook Bald had considered himself fortunate indeed when he had noticed this far superior pair sticking out of the bin and had wasted no time in claiming them as his own.

In addition to this visual appraisal of the prawnman the Visitor struggled to place the faint unpleasant aroma that seemed to hang in the air between them. He was sure he had encountered that smell before. But where? And when? That the aroma was faint was due to the efforts of Master Miles. Following his agreement with the Visitor the previous day the thought had occurred that strangers to the town sometimes experienced difficulty in breathing when they first encountered one of the Prawning Fleets' crewmen. With this in mind Boathook Bald had been summoned to the courtyard of his employer's home and, upon arrival, had been hosed down, scrubbed with a stiff yard broom and then hosed down a second time for good measure. Satisfied that this should be sufficient to smooth over the worst of the man's noxious edges, the Master then explained what would be required of him when meeting with the Visitor; "Tell him a few of our old customs Bald, and some of our poems too."

This had been the instruction which had caused Boathook Bald to launch enthusiastically into a weather forecasting doggerel before the Visitor even had time to introduce himself properly. The glass of rum, as Master Miles had carefully explained, would be a very fitting method of encouraging conversation in the crewman. Before partaking of the liquid, however, a fresh thought seemed to get between his lips and the glass:

"That's one o' our oldest rhymes," he declared grandly, "an' it's one o' the first things we learn, 'undreds and 'undreds o' years ago the very first local prawnman thought up that rhyme. When the second local prawnman come along 'e learned it off the first y'see. Then the third learned it off the second an' then 'e was able t' teach it t' the fourth. So it went on, an' that's 'ow it is we all learned it."

Nodding with satisfaction, the prawnman raised the glass to his lips. The Visitor, wishing to keep the conversation going, said,

"It is rather similar to that old shepherds' rhyming couplet."

A remark which resulted in his shirt being instantly sprayed with the mouthful of rum that Boathook Bald had been about to swallow.

"They nicked it off us, them shep'erds," shouted the prawnman. Sitting upright in a posture of indignation he began licking the rum from his beard and fingers.

"Them shep'erds! One of 'em come into the town once an' 'eard us sayin' it an' 'e nicked it off us an' 'e told it t' all the other shep'erds."

Shocked by the outburst which he had inadvertently caused, the Visitor attempted an apology, but it fell on deaf ears.

"That's why your local prawnman don't like shep'erds y'see," continued Boathook Bald in a calmer tone, staring regretfully at the rum now being absorbed into the visitor's shirt. "Nasty 'orrible little buggers they are. But we gets 'em back for it, oh yes, we gets 'em back good an' proper!"

The Visitor waited for the next part of this narrative. After a minute he realised that this was not forthcoming and a little prompting seemed to be required.

"So," he asked, "how do you get back at the shepherds?"

"That's a nice drop o' rum that is. Trouble is though, the glass got itself empty afore I finished drinkin' it," replied Boathook Bald, his eyes fixed upon the empty glass and his mind fixed upon the sort of prompting that was required.

"Y'might as well get a bottle," he added as the Visitor stood up to go into the nearby New Inn, "it'll save on y'r legs."

If the Visitor had any misgivings about the amount of money he was going to have to spend on drink, it did not show in his smile as he handed his informant the bottle of rum. With the briefest of 'thank yous' the prawnman unscrewed the cap and filled up his glass. He then took a generous swig from the bottle, pulled a face that suggested he was trying to swallow a live crab and, after replacing the cap, tucked the bottle into one of his waders. He was then ready to carry on with his story:

"Sometimes the fishin' is down, not many prawns out there gettin' into our pots y'see, we spends more time out at sea with less t' show for it. So then there is less food at 'ome 'cos we can't go an' buy much. That's the way fishin' 'as always been. Now then, mos' fishermen jus' 'ave t' go 'ungry, but your prawnman don't. We figure that if them shep'erds reckon it's alright t'come 'ere an' nick our rhymes then it's ok for us t' go there an' nick their sheeps. That's like, fair exchange."

Glancing at the Visitor Boathook Bald noticed a frown of disapproval so, before continuing, he took a large gulp from the glass of rum and pushed the bottle further down into his wader.

"Well, that seems fair 'nough to us anyway. But it aint the

job o' the prawnman t'go an' get a sheep, it's 'is wife an' daughter's job. Now I bet y'never knew that, did you?

The Visitor admitted that no, he did not know that, which caused his informant to smile triumphantly and to drain the rest of the rum from his glass.

"There's a very good reason for that," he declared whilst apparently trying to swallow a couple more live crabs, "an' that's 'cos y'r prawnman can't sing whereas y'r fishwife can."

A dark cloud passed over the sun and, momentarily distracted, the pair glanced up at the sky.

"It looks like it may rain later," commented the Visitor.

Boathook Bald lifted his head and looked to the west. He then sniffed the air, glanced up at the seagulls circling overhead and announced;

"No, it'll be clear in a couple o' 'ours." which caused the Visitor, mistaking the prawnman's undying optimism for inbred wisdom in forecasting the weather, to be very impressed.

"An' that," continued Boathook Bald "is why the prawnin' families 'ave got sheep stealin' shanties, Y'see sheeps are very timid, so when the fishwife takes 'er boys up t' the field at night the sheeps will run away t' the other end o' the field. So what 'appens is they all sits down an' sings-very quiet an' gentle-some o' the special sheep stealin' shanties. After an 'our o'this the sheeps calm down an' gets used to 'em, they'll ignore the fishwife an' 'er boys. Then, when a sheep gets close 'nough, the boys'll jump on it an' ...."

"Wait a moment," interrupted the Visitor "I thought you said it was the daughters that went with their mother to the fields! I would have thought the sons would have been with their fathers, learning the ways of the sea."

"Ah, that's right. Y'see, all of our kids are called 'boys' 'til they reach their early teens. Obviously that makes it easier f'r ev'ryone. Then the girls become the mothers' boys an' the sons become the fathers' boys. Then that lasts 'til they grows the lumps 'n' bumps that says they're a man or a woman y'see."

Although this answer did little to enlighten the Visitor he decided to let the subject pass. In spite of being able to follow the logic behind the prawnman's justification for their rustling of sheep he knew that a court would view the matter differently. For this reason it was an area of the prawning community's life that would be of no use to his research: it was illegal and therefore unusable when he got back to his office. But the prawnman's relating the details of this activity did serve to relax his tongue, which suited the Visitor's purpose perfectly. From long experience he had learned that these preliminary conversations generally contained nothing of use to him, he had to allow his subject to warm up first. What he really wanted to know about were the traditions imbued in each community, the eccentricities and quirks that made such people unique in their ways. This information, to his employers, was a marketable commodity. What he was waiting for, when it arrived, came out of the sky on the wings of a large seagull which landed on the ground close to where they were sitting.

The gull was carrying a young eel in its beak which, when dropped upon the ground, proved to be very much alive and clearly averse to the notion of being eaten. Out of its natural element, the fight for survival caused the eel to writhe and contort its length into a series of different postures – all the time watched by its predator who danced around it taking the occasional peck at the victim in order to tire it into submission. The seagull knew it had only a limited time in which to complete this process, just as he had stolen this fish from a smaller bird so might a larger one come and relieve him of his meal. The seagull's dance was therefore interspersed with furtive glances skywards. Meanwhile his pecks at the eel soon became more vicious and frantic until, torn and bloodied, it finally lay still.

The two men had fallen silent as they watched this scenario: the prawnman with the detachment of one who had seen the same act played out many times before and the Visitor with the eyes of one who, although he did not want to witness the outcome, could not tear his gaze from this example of nature's grotesque reality. His tender sensibilities were rescued from this dilemma by Boathook Bald suddenly speaking the words that the Visitor had been waiting to hear;

"See that gull? That's a Blackback that is. There's one o' our traditions 'bout them birds."

Here the prawnman leaned forward and, pulling a bottle of rum out from inside one of his waders, replenished his glass. The Visitor noted that he used a different bottle, taken from the other wader, than the one he had recently purchased for the prawnman. However, before this train of thought could lead the Visitor into calculating exactly how many bottles of rum the waders could possibly contain Boathook Bald, after a sip at the now full glass, continued.

"When we are out there on the prawnin' grounds, we always sees one or two o'them birds sat on the rocks, jus' watching us. Now then, it is our belief that these birds contains the souls o'the ol' Prawnin' Masters y'see. After the ol' men dies off they comes back as Blackbacks an' they keeps an eye on the Prawnin' Fleet y'see, t' make sure we're all kept safe. An' when we aint out there they keeps an eye on our pots f'r us."

"What a lovely notion," observed the Visitor.

"Well, I can't say as I knows what a notion is, beggin' your pardon. But don't y'go thinkin' I'm makin' all this up, it's our tradition y'see. All I do know is that it's a great comfort t' me knowin' the ol' Prawnin' Masters are lookin' out f'r me. O'course, I ain't a Master so I won't come back as one o'them birds. I'm a crewman an' we got a diff'rent tradition f'r when we dies. We comes back as ragworms y'see."

"Ragworms? What on earth is a ragworm?" asked the Visitor.

"Don't you know?" Boathook Bald took a great gulp of rum in his surprise at the Visitor's ignorance. He then set his mind to trying to describe this creature.

"Well you won't find it in the earth 'cos it lives in the mud on the seabed. You gets little ones an' you gets big ones, all dependin' on their size y'see. They looks like any other worm 'cept they got these wriggly bits all up an' down their body an' their 'eads is diff'rent too."

Boathook Bald was floundering now, never before in his life having been called upon to describe a ragworm. As luck would have it, however, at that moment a cat walked past them. Inspired, the Prawnman pointed towards its retreating form.

"See that cats' arse?" He turned to the Visitor "That's what the 'ead of a ragworm looks like! O'course, if I 'ad a choice, I'd rather come back lookin' like a Blackback. Lovely birds they are, though between you 'n' me I 'ave 'eard they got some filthy 'abits. But they're better t'look at than a ragworm an' that's a fact. Mind you, Master Miles says that if I come back lookin' like a ragworm then that'll be a great improvement on 'ow I looks now. But I reckon 'e only says that t'be kind t'me."

"Tell me," asked the Visitor, suddenly feeling a great urge to turn the prawnman's attention away from the subject of ragworms, "do you have any other traditions in the Fleet about death?"

"D'you mean like what 'appened when Ol' Bluey White lowered 'is 'ook f' the las' time?"

"Lowered his hook?"

"Yeah. Meanin' 'e died 'cos that's what we says when one of us dies. Lower your 'ook, it's like droppin' the anchor y'see."

A nod from the Visitor confirmed that this is exactly what he meant and so the prawnman continued; "Well then, 'e was a Master y'see. So the first thing that 'appens is all the other Masters, the ones what ain't died, all gets t'gether an' draws lots. That's t'see which one of 'em goes an' comforts the widow. Y'know, tell 'er what a great bloke 'e was an' all that other stuff they likes t'be told. While 'e's doin' that all the other Masters 'ave a race in their boats. So when Bluey died that was called 'Blueys' Race'"

"How unusual. A race in his honour." The Visitor had never heard of anything like this before and it alerted his professional instincts. At last, he felt, he was hearing something of real substance - a tradition peculiar to this community.

"No. It's a race t'get out t'the prawnin' grounds. T'see which one of 'em c'n grab as many of Blueys' pots as they can. Pots cost money y'see an' they knows a dead man ain't goin' t' need 'em for 'imself anymore. So, as they suddenly belongs t'nobody, they're up f'r grabs."

Shocked beyond belief at this unexpected, and seemingly callous, twist in the prawnman's story the Visitor could say nothing. Boathook Bald, mistaking the silence for appreciation, took a sip of rum and continued:

"So that's a tradition I suppose. 'nother one is this; when a crewman gets cremated, 'e always does it with 'is clothes on. So that saves the widow from havin' t' build a bonfire in the garden t' burn 'em separate – an' it keeps all the smell up at the crem y'see. And o'course the dead man always gets 'is poem."

"Gets his poem?"

"Ah, that's right. Then after the crem we ….."

"Hold on a moment," the Visitor interrupted, "what do you mean by "getting his poem"?

"Well, some o'the fishin' folks 'ave songs that've been written for 'em. We don't get songs cos we can't sing, so we 'ave poems instead. We 'ave poems for everythin': gettin' born, gettin' married, gettin' dead. That's 'ow our traditions is 'anded down y'see. An' we've got our weather forecastin' ones that we learns when we are little, like that red sky one that the shep'erds nicked, 'ere's 'nother one:

> When the wind's in the West,
> The prawnin' is best,
> When the wind's in the East,
> The prawnin' is least,
> With a Southerly blow,
> The prawnin' goes slow,
> An' when the wind's in the North
> The prawns bugger off.

We 'ave a poem for everythin' y'see"

"But what about prawnmens' shanties?" the Visitor asked. "Surely you must have some of those when you are out on the boat working."

"If I went an' started singin' when I was in the boat Master Miles would 'ave somethin' t'say 'bout it f'r a start." replied the prawnman firmly. "Well, 'e wouldn't say anythin' 'bout it at all – 'e'd jus' belt me aroun' the 'ead with an oar. An' that would be my own fault f'r doin' the singin'. As I said jus' now, y'r prawnman can't sing an' if we trys it then folks get angry with us!"

"But the prawnmen must have their sea shanties," the Visitor insisted, "all fishermen have them, don't they?"

"News t'me if they do!" stated Boathook Bald "I'll 'ave t' think 'bout that one" Taking the opportunity to leave off talking for a few minutes, the prawnman indulged in some very serious drinking from the glass of rum. When he found himself ready to speak again it was in the manner of one who had searched his memory thoroughly and had discovered little of substance to impart.

"I think the nearest thing we got to a shanty is sometimes when I pulls up one o'our lobster pots. The Master 'as a couple of those out on the off chance 'e might catch a bluey, meanin' a lobster, f'r 'imself. 'e's rather partial t' the taste but not partial to payin' f'r one y'see. So if a pot comes up with a bluey in it then I will sing the word "Lobster" over an' over a few times. 'cos I knows Master Miles will be too 'appy t' hit me if I do a bit o' the singin' then. But that ain't really a shanty as such. I reckon that if y'eard 'bout fishermen singin' in their boats then it mus' be the ones who sings the 'ymns"

"Singing hymns while they are working!" the Visitor was rather taken with this idea and the pleasure showed in his expression "What a wonderful thought."

"All very well you sayin' that," grumbled the prawnman "y'don't 'ave t' listen to 'em! They drives y'bloody mad after an 'our or so of it. Y'see, it ain't the ones who goes t' the big church that do it, them's quite 'appy t'give the Lord 'is one day a week an' keep the other six f'r 'emselves. It's the others, the ones who go t' the pecul'ar little churches. Them what carries it aroun' with 'em seven days a week an' don't shut up 'bout it. They sings out in their boats but it ain't shanties, it's bloody 'ymns! I've 'eard that their kids c'n sing 'ymns afore they learns t' talk! My mate Fiddler Crabbe reckons that's 'cos the parents are bangin' out a few verses of '*Onward Christian Soldiers*' while they're on the job an' makin' the little buggers."

Although not being a church-goer the Visitor had attended schools where Religious Education had mainly focussed on the teachings of the Bible. This insistent yet incomplete learning of the Christian faith now led him to being unsure of whether or not his informant was committing a blasphemy. It has to be said that, despite not being an adherent of any particular religion, the Visitor still carried such a strong image of Hell in his mind that he did not wish to risk going there. In order to steer the prawnman away from this uncertain area he asked;

"Fiddler Crabbe? Is he a prawnman too?"

"Ol' Fid? Y'won't catch 'im goin' out in a boat!" Boathook Bald spoke as one declaring a universal truth. "'e's got 'is work cut out keepin' all the Puritans under control."

The prawnman then threw back his head and let out a great roar of laughter. The Visitor, although aware that the conversation was heading once more into dangerous territory for his immortal soul, felt himself excluded from a private joke. Quite naturally he wanted to know more and signalled this wish with the raising of an eyebrow.

"Well," Boathook Bald was obviously willing to let the Visitor know of Fiddler Crabbe's history, "it all goes back 'undreds an' 'undreds o'years. At one time the Crabbe fam'ly was all prawners, men an' boys. It's their claim that they 'ad the mos' boats, the bes' boats an' the bigges' catches, they reckon at one time they 'ad the 'ole fishery sewn up an' nobody else could get a look in. Mind you, if y'believe 'alf o'what they say you'd be thinkin' they built the 'ole town an' populated it on their days off! An' then they'll follow that by reck'nin' that it's only down t' the Crabbes that the tide goes in an' out an' that the sun rises in the sky ev'ry mornin'. They're a gobby bunch an' ol' Fid knows it. I've told 'im as much many a time, like mates can. But anyway, they don't none of 'em go out prawnin' anymore. Not f'r manys the year."

"So," the Visitor was intrigued, "what happened to cause them to stop prawning? It must have been something quite serious."

"Ah, now then, that was all down t' the Puritans y'see." explained the prawnman, "When prawnmen 'as been away at sea f'r a while an' then they comes ashore they gets the lan' sickness......."

"Land sickness?" interrupted the Visitor. He wondered if the prawnman was deliberately spinning him a yarn, "I have never heard of such a thing?"

"Well we gets it whether you've 'eard of it or not!" declared Boathook Bald, his tone conveying defiance at any further doubt, "Bein' ashore, it's like walkin' aroun' on somethin' that don't move all the time an' that don't feel nat'ral. When y' walks through town it's like the pavement is bangin' on the soles o' y'r feet. Then after a few days o' this y' starts noticin' the dirt. Bein' ashore is very dirty 'cos y'aint got the spray washin' everythin' down all the time like y'do on a boat. An' it ain't like 'onest dirt, the sort y'jus' live with - it's lan' dirt an' it gets t'y'worse in a way, dunno why. They do say that the only way t'get rid of it is with bloody soap! An' then y'starts noticin' y'been feelin' out of sorts f'r a few days an' y' knows y'ain't goin' to get better 'til y'gets out in a boat again. O'course once y'do get in a boat again it's 'cos y'got t'work, so then y'can't wait f'r the trip t' be over an' t'get back ashore. Master Miles says the sea is both a curse an' a blessin'. 'e says that's the way it's always been f'r sailors an' it always will be 'til the day the seas run dry!"

The Visitor wanted to tell the prawnman that, during the course of his work, he had been constantly amazed at how fishermen accepted the harshness of their lot in life. Not only this, they could also express this acceptance in terms that were almost poetical. However, as he did not have the right words to say this, instead he asked;

"So what has this to do with the Crabbe family's decision to stop prawning?"

"Ah, well, the one sure way o'delayin' the start of the lan' sickness is to get y'self into an ale'ouse as quick as y'can - drinkin' bein' the best cure f'r it y'see. So it was that a few 'undred years ago the Prawnin' Fleet all comes ashore, 'eaded across the quay t' skull a few ales an' discovered all the ale'ouses shut down. It was all down t' the local Puritans y'see, they'd got it into their 'eads that drinkin' was bad an' their God didn't like folks doin' it. Bloody daft they were I says! So then the Prawnin' Fleet, an' most of 'em Crabbes, done the only thing that they could do an' started a riot."

Making a quick lunge at his glass of rum, the prawnman took a great gulp before continuing with the tale.

"Stories of that day are still told in the town, they gets 'anded down from father t' son an' from mother t' daughter. 'tis said that this is t'serve as a warnin' o' what 'appens when folks start interferin' with the nat'ral order o' things y'see. Anyways, the riot went on an' on 'til them that 'ad the ale'ouses shut down knew that they would 'ave t' get them opened up again. The town would've got ruined otherwise 'cos prawnmen are alright so long as y' don't upset 'em too much. Them Puritans 'ad to learn that the 'ard way but once they learned it they soon let the ale'ouses open again!"

At this point Boathook Bald's face broke into a huge triumphant grin as if he and he alone had been the key instrument in this change of policy. Then whether due to the quantity of rum that he had imbibed or because he was warming to a theme (and the Visitor felt very strongly that it was the former) as he continued he became very animated with his gestures. With one arm he pointed along the quay towards a lifting bridge while the other arm made a sweeping motion as if encompassing the whole town.

"If y'go an' look on that bridge," he announced grandly, "y'will see the town crest an' it's got some Latin words on it. One o'the first things that we gets told when we are kids is what them words mean in English - it's 'Accordin' t' the Custom o' the Town' is what it says. It means that strangers are made welcome but they aint t' try an' change 'ow we do things 'ere. An' if they aint 'appy with that then they c'n piss off!"

He banged a fist down on the bench beside him, thus putting an official stamp on this declaration. The Visitor, feeling both shocked and delighted at this speech, could only exclaim;

"And quite right too!"

Then, suddenly finding himself embarrassed at the force with which he had said this, he quickly sought refuge in the matter in hand.

"But," he continued in a calmer tone, "what has all of this to do with Fiddler Crabbe never going out in a boat?"

"Well, accordin' t' Fid, once the ale'ouses was all opened up the Crabbes got t'gether an' vowed that they would never ever put t' sea again. Just in case they got back from a voyage an' discovered that the Puritans 'ad been up t'more dirty tricks as soon as their backs was turned. The Crabbes figured that keepin' an eye on the ale'ouses was a lot more important than catchin' prawns y'see."

"There are not really any such things as Puritans nowadays though." the Visitor pointed out, "At least, not as they were all those years ago."

"Y'try tellin' Fiddler Crabbe that!" responded Boathook Bald, "'e'd say 'You may not be able t'see any Puritans but I knows they're out there. Y' could talk 'til y're blue in the face, ol' Fid reckons 'e knows best on that one. It nearly got us all locked up once y'know."

Reaching down into one of his waders the prawnman pulled forth a chunk of bread. He inspected it closely, removed a few bits of green mould and then took a bite from it. The Visitor, too polite to do otherwise, stared straight ahead and pretended that this was not happening. After washing his quick snack down with a sip of rum and pushing the remainder of the bread back into a wader, Boathook Bald then carried on with his story. Whilst doing so he once again became highly animated with his gestures.

"We was sat in the 'Towns Arms' down on the quay there. Suddenly Fid looks out o'the window an' shouts 'Look out! Puritans!'"

The prawnman jumped to his feet and performed a very passable pantomime of a man in a state of panic;

"'Quick', shouts Fid, 'barricade the doors.' An' with that 'e starts chargin' roun' the bar grabbin' at tables an' chairs an' pilin' 'em up 'gainst the door. Ol' Vin, 'e's the Lan'lord y'see, 'e was gettin' in a right ol' state tryin' t' shut Fid up an' calm 'im down."

Here Boathook Bald acted out both the principle roles- Fiddler Crabbe building the barricade and Old Vin trying to stop him. This energetic charade caused the prawnmans already drink flushed features to redden even further. Of a sudden all movement ceased and he turned to face the Visitor.

"Oh it was a right t'do an' no mistake 'bout that! Trouble was, it were two o'clock in the mornin' an' Ol' Vin was givin' us a lock in. An' what Fid 'ad seen out the window wasn't no Puritans at all, it was the local constables doin' their rounds. 'im doin' that 'ad attracted their attention on us y'see. It was lucky that they was partial to a drink 'emselves, Ol' Vin smoothed the 'ole thing over by givin' 'em a few brandies t' keep out the night air. An' then they went away with jus' tellin' us we wasn't really supposed t' be drinkin' at that time o'night."

Then, like a strong wind sharply dropping to a breeze with the turning of the tide, Boathook Bald took his seat and carried on with his tale in more subdued tones; "O'course Fid don't spend all 'is time lookin' out for Puritans, though 'e's always got 'alf an eye on who's goin' in the ale'ouses. 'e's one o'our musicians an' on that account 'e never wants for a meal or a few cups o'cider. We always figures that if someone can turn out a tune an' liven up our lives then we got t' look after 'em. An' that's why Fid is jus' as much a part o'the Prawnin' Fleet as if 'e was out there liftin' the pots with us."

"He sounds like quite a fascinating character," observed the Visitor, "I'd like to meet him sometime."

"Y'already 'ave," replied the prawnman, "though y' weren't t' know it was 'im. When y' first arrived in the town an' was askin' about us prawnmen we didn't know who y'was. So we sent Fid off t' find you an' work out if y' was from the Gov'ment or not. Sometimes the Gov'ment try an' find out what we're up to an' see if they c'n get some shillin's out of us. Or they try an' make them as got kids send 'em to school. It was Fid that managed t' work out that y' was one of those others, the ones what wants t'find out about our way o'life for the telly people or somethin'."

"But I didn't tell anybody why I was here," protested the

Visitor, "not that it was a secret of course. It's because my conversations with people didn't seem to get that far."

"Y'don't need t' tell Fid nothin', 'e can work out what folks is up to without them tellin' 'im! Says it's somethin' in their manner." The prawnman, completely unaware that his revelations were having quite a profound effect upon his listener, was giving his tongue free rein. "F'r instance, if y' was from the Gov'ment then 'ow y'spoke to people would've been a bit sterner. Y'was too p'lite for that y'see. So we worked out y'was one of 'em other ones, the ones who jus' want t'know about us. Y'was lucky too! Normally y'see we don't talk to 'em, y're the first one that we 'ave spoke to."

Starting to realise that his earlier difficulties with making contact with his subject had been a carefully orchestrated plan on their part, the Visitor was shocked. He could only ask;

"So why the change of heart? Why did you decide to talk to me?"

Boathook Bald threw the visitor a look that made it clear he was holding a great secret, yet one that he could not contain. When he spoke it was as one who was taking another into his confidence.

"Ah, well. Master Miles says we might be livin' in a quiet little backwater but that don't mean we don't know what goes on in the world. In the ol' days when folks come and asked us questions they was just a nuis'nce. There was us tryin' t'get on with our work, say I was paintin' the boat down on the 'ard for example. One of 'em would come up an' say 'Hello, is that a boat?' jus' t' get a conv'sation goin' y'see. An' if I was t' answer 'em an' say "Yes" that would give 'em the confidence t' ask 'nother daft question. So then they would say "Are you paintin' it ?" and so on. Drive y'bloody mad they would! So it was always easier t' jus' ignore 'em 'til they went away.

But then there's people like you who come an' ask questions an' the next thing that anyone knows is that it's on the telly! Master Miles says to me 'Bald,' 'e says 'the way the fishin' is goin' these days it won't be long afore we c'n make more money out o' talkin' 'bout it than by goin' out there an' doin' it'. So then all the Prawnin' Masters got t'gether an' decided 'mongst 'emselves that they wasn't goin' t' speak t' no more telly people 'less they got a few shillin's out of it."

"He got a bit more than a few shillings out of me." murmured the Visitor. At the same time he wondered if the prawnman had ever heard of decimal currency or if 'shillings' was just a colloquial term for money in general in this part of the world.

"Ah, I know that. That's why Master Miles said I 'ad t'be p'lite t' you 'an tell you all 'bout our customs an' traditions. 'e said that was the least we could do seein' as 'ow the quids y' gave 'im was goin' to buy 'im a new uniform. What with 'im bein' the Admiral o'the Prawnin' Fleet 'e's got t' look better than all the other Masters y'see, an' uniforms don't come cheap."

At this point it suddenly occurred to Boathook Bald that perhaps he was speaking rather too freely to the Visitor about the financial dealings undertaken with Master Miles. So, with a look that was almost accusing and a tone of voice almost sharp, he said:

"Anyways, what you an' Master Miles does with y'r money is none o'my business!" And in this manner made it clear not only that the subject was closed, but also that the Visitor was somehow at fault for any possible indiscretions.

For a while the two men sat in silence: one drinking from his glass of rum, the other trying to decide upon his next line of enquiry. The Visitor needed to work out how to direct his questioning in order to produce the best results for use back in the office and, at that present moment, he had to admit that he was struggling to do so. As they sat a passer-by, dressed very similarly to the prawnman, walked past them and nodded a greeting to Boathook Bald – a greeting which was ignored until he had passed out of earshot and then only acknowledged by a sneer.

"See 'im?"

The Visitor felt his arm being nudged and he looked in the direction indicated by his companion.

"'e likes t'play the prawnman 'e does, but we all reckons 'is fam'ly was into the shrimpin'. 'e aint no proper prawnman!"

"What is the difference?" enquired the Visitor who, like most people, could never distinguish a shrimp from a prawn.

"Shrimps are stupid!" This answer came promptly and firmly. "An' so are shrimpmen!"

The Visitor found himself at a loss as how to respond to this information. On the one hand he did not wish to offend the prawnman, on the other he did not feel that his question had been answered. The inward struggle he experienced, knowing that the matter was irrelevant but with his curiosity frustratingly whetted, did not last long however. It soon became clear that Boathook Bald had more to say on the subject.

"We makes jokes up 'bout the shrimpmen. Like we says they sleeps with cormorants 'cos it's the only way they ever goin' t'ave a shag! Like the shrimps they're stupid. More stupid! Your prawn is quite brainy y'see, sometimes they leads us a right merry jig afore we gets 'em in our pots. But shrimps, they queue up t' go in the nets t' get 'emselves eaten. Daft sods! An' the shrimpmen got this stupid in 'em too, it's all down t' that stupid an' the bony part that we don't 'ave shrimpmen 'ere anymore."

"Bony part?" The Visitor, not for the first time that day, was confused, "What is the bony part? What does it mean?"

"That ol' Frenchie, Napoleon." Boathook Bald was incredulous that the Visitor appeared to have never heard of the man. He took a sip of rum then, remembering that city dwellers were sometimes ignorant of subjects close to the heart of sea folk, decided to fill this gap in his companion's education.

"Years an' years ago, afore I was born, the Gov'ment was 'avin' a war with France y'see. It was 'cos this bloke Bony Part wanted t' come over t' England an' be in charge of us an' we didn't want that. Now then, that war wasn't good f'r us f'r two reasons: firstly 'cos the Gov'ment wanted all the fishermen t' sign up for the Navy but mainly 'cos it was interferin' with the smugglin'. All them Navy ships snoopin' 'bout in the channel y'see. It was ok if a Frenchie Navy ship come across an English smuggler, once they knew who it was an' what they was up to they'd let 'em go. It were an import'nt trade for the Frenchie merchants over there y'see. But our Navy would've seized the ship an' put all of the crew into man o'war ships. Then no smugglin' would've got done an' everyone would've lost out."

"But Bonaparte intended to invade this country, he needed to be stopped."

The Visitor, uncomfortable with what appeared to be an unpatriotic view, felt the need to point out this fact to the prawnman. Boathook Bald, however, dismissed the Visitor's objection with an impatient wave of his hand.

"If 'e 'ad alanded 'ere 'e'd've got kicked out, y'c'n be sure o' that! An' a lot o'our men did sign up t'fight 'im, you c'n be sure o'that too. But the rest of 'em 'ad the smugglin' t' take care of."

He held up his glass of rum. "Once you start puttin' taxes on this stuff it buggers up the taste an' that's a fact!"

The Visitor could see that the conversation was moving towards an argument that he had no chance of winning. Nor did he want to pursue it. Instead, wishing to get back to the original line of enquiry, he asked Boathook Bald what had happened to all the shrimpmen of that time: had they gone to fight the war and not returned? However, before the prawnman had the opportunity to reply to this, there came the sound of a disturbance from within a nearby alehouse. As the pair turned their heads in the direction of the commotion the suspected shrimpman was seen to leave the premises, projected head first through an open window. The prawnman pointed at the somewhat battered figure as he pulled himself up out of the gutter;

"Well," he said, "there's y'r answer t'that one! That's what 'appens to a shrimpman when 'e tries t'do the fightin'! No, they all died out 'cos o' their stupidity. What 'appened was this: back in the days o' the Press Gangs our men was luckier than most. There's only two ways a Press could approach the town y'see. If they come by lan' they'd've 'ad t'cross over the 'eath, an' if they came by sea then they'd've 'ad t' come up the 'arbour. Either way they'd've been seen long afore they got 'ere an' so the men 'ad time to 'ide from 'em. Now then, one o'the tricks used by the fishermen was t' get 'emselves into one o'the little bays further up the 'arbour. Lots o'reed beds up there y'see. So they'd cut 'emselves a length o' reed an' then lay down in the shallows, where it was jus' deep 'nough t' cover their bodies. They couldn't be seen by nobody an' they 'ad the reed t' breathe through y'see. An' then when the Press was gone one o'the womenfolks would go an' tell 'em it was all clear.

Now then, they do say that once when this 'ad 'appened they all stood up after gettin' the ok, all of 'em 'cept the shrimpmen. An' that was 'cos they was drowneded y'see. The daft sods 'ad cut twigs 'stead of reeds! O'course then they couldn't breathe under the water so that's what drowneded 'em an' they do say that's why we ain't got shrimpmen 'ere anymore. O'course there's some o' their families still 'roun' the town, but we can spot 'em a mile off an' we gives 'em a wide berth."

Then, with a glance towards the quay and a pause to drain the rest of the rum from his glass, the prawnman suddenly jumped to his feet;

"Anyways," he said "I can't talk t'y'no more t'day. I got t'go an' catch a mack'rel."

"You fish for mackerel as well?" asked the Visitor.

"Only one," came the reply. "It's 'nother one of our traditions y'see. At this time o'year, after we signed on with a Master f'r a season, we c'n use 'is boat t' go an' catch a mack'rel each."

"Have you not just the time to tell me about this tradition?" The Visitor's tone was almost pleading. Before answering the prawnman glanced over at the quay once again.

"I'll 'ave t'be quick 'bout it," he stated firmly "I got t' catch the tide. With Master Miles I c'n use the boat but I aint t'use the engine. I 'as t' row it out on the oars an' it's an 'eavy ol' bugger. If I don't get the tide up me arse I'll never do it! Not much t' tell anyway. This time o'year when the mack'rel starts comin' in down at the entrance t'the 'arbour we all goes an' catches ourselves one. Then we 'as t' get it 'ome as quick as we can, afore it dies y'see. Then we puts it in the bath so we c'n fatten it up, that's f'r our Christmas dinner y'see."

"So how do you have a bath between now and Christmas?"

Even as he asked this question, the natural response to one so fastidious in matters of cleanliness, the Visitor knew that the answer to it would be something quite alien to his ears. At that instant he also remembered where he had previously encountered the faint smell that the prawnman carried about him: the pile of rags in the ruined boat!

"Oh, that's no problem, it's one o' the traditions in the Prawnin' Fleet that the Masters lets us 'ave some time off on Boxin' Day. Only we don't call it that, we calls it 'Bath Day'. Anyways, I really 'ave got t' go now or I'll be buggered with the tide."

"Can we meet up again tomorrow? I would like to hear more," the Visitor asked as, waders clanking with an indeterminate number of bottles, the prawnman moved off in the direction of the Fisherman's Dock.

"If y're 'appy t' buy me drinks then I'm 'appy t'talk! I'll be 'ere same time as I was t'day." Boathook Bald called back over his shoulder.

Chapter Five

The Visitor, following his first meeting with Boathook Bald, had returned to his lodgings. Upon entering the house, a modest mid-terrace property situated in the town's High Street, he had detected a faint smell of pipe tobacco. He briefly wondered about where this aroma could have originated from and whether another lodger had taken up residence. It was certainly the first time that he had been aware of tobacco smoke since his arrival there a week ago. As for the brand of tobacco, he knew this immediately. It was the same as his father had smoked, a very distinctive pungent blend which once encountered was not to be forgotten. Its presence in the lodging house that morning gave the Visitor cause for reflection: a slight pang of sorrow for the loss of his father coupled with a reminder about the uniform that hung upstairs in the wardrobe. Without delay the Visitor went to his room to once again don his father's Merchant Navy uniform. This was his one obsession, a secret vice which he was unable to relinquish. For although he felt a little self conscious arrayed in this smart attire, knowing in truth he had not earned the right to wear it, at the same time it felt good.

His father had been a ship's Captain, as had the male line of his family for many generations. As a child the Visitor would look forward to his father's all too brief periods of shore leave, occasions when it seemed the family home took on a whole new atmosphere. Gone was the genteel peace that reigned when life evolved around mother and son alone, in its place a hectic race for the three of them to do as much as possible together in the short time allotted. Visits to far-flung relatives, where he would play football with older cousins who treated him as a favoured younger brother, would be interspersed with family days out. The young lad's first choice was to be taken to a wildlife park for here he could see animals from all over the world. It made him very proud to think that his father sailed his ship to the countries where these beasts lived in the open. In the evenings he would be allowed to stay up late and would sit enthralled as stories of his grandfather's and great-grandfather's exploits in the days of sail were related to him. These were tales which only his father knew about, for no other elder in his world ever spoke of them. And as he listened, his imagination running wild, he would study his father's face whilst visualising his words as an exciting reality: a stormy sea sending heavy waves crashing along the length of the deck, sails cracking loudly as they were caught by the wind. And at the helm his father calmly guiding the ship through the tempest, his smart uniform remaining unruffled as he puffed contentedly on his pipe. But no, his father would tell him gently when the boy spoke of these flights of fancy, times have changed. Sail had given way to steam and with this evolution in the mode of propulsion the skills of the sailor had adapted accordingly. Whilst the sea still remained a force to be reckoned with, then so did the men who would master it in order to see their ships brought safely into port. And, it was emphasised, this was the family tradition to aspire to: it was an ancestry to be proud of. A ship's Captain had to rise to any challenge - be it from the weather or a new method of handling his vessel. It had been their ability to rise to these challenges which had made their family name one to be respected in the maritime world. That his father was telling him these things as he expected the boy to follow in this family tradition never once entered the lad's head.

The Visitor, at that young age, enjoyed these stories simply because of who it was telling them to him. When his father was away on a voyage the boy's life was dominated by women - his mother, his aunts, his grandmothers - and to have just sporadic and short periods of male company could only be a fascination to him, not an influence. The shadowy figure who wandered in and out of his life had merely taken on a mythological existence within an impressionable mind. Thus, when he spoke of his father to school friends it was of his ship being attacked by giant whales or sea serpents. Also there would be fantasies of battles with ruthless swashbuckling pirates - battles that ended with the cruel barbarians getting their just deserts as they floundered in shark infested waters. On other occasions the pirates would win, but this was only when his father had turned pirate in order to sail in search of buried treasure. That this part-time patriarch completely disappeared for five years shortly after the boy's tenth birthday only served to fuel the myth. The absence of any reference to the reason as to why his father no longer came home gave him plenty of room for conjecture. Whispered conversations between his elders, his mother shedding tears that she was unaware of him noticing, all contributed to his reluctance to ask questions. At first the childhood ingenuity saw his father in prison for acts of piracy but this was, with more mature reasoning, eventually abandoned. In its stead was the knowledge that something had gone amiss with his parents marriage, intelligence that had reached him via overhearing his mother, in a rare passion, making reference to 'that bloody slut' whist talking about his father's disappearance to her sister.

When his parents resumed their married life they, publicly at least, did so with as little fuss as possible. It was as if nothing had happened: so complete was this illusion that they did not even tell their only child that his father had returned. One day after school the youngster walked into the house to be greeted by the familiar aroma of pipe tobacco and the sight of his father's peaked cap upon the hatstand. Walking cautiously into the living room he was greeted by the sight of his parents relaxing on the sofa with cups of tea in their hands, they smiled their welcomes at him as if this scenario was nothing other than the one which he normally found upon his return home each afternoon. From that day on they were a family once again with any indiscretions committed by a wayward sailor consigned to history. If the father did have cause to feel punished for his infidelity it was in the loss of his son's place in the family heritage. For as the lad approached school leaving age it had become more than apparent that he was not cut out for life at sea. The over-protected existence that he had become used to, spoilt by the women around him who had nobody else to molly-coddle, in turn prevented him from developing that most needed quality in a sailor: commonsense.

His father recognised this fact with great personal sadness; "The idiot would not even make cabin boy," was the harsh judgement passed by this last in a long line of Sea Captains. Though deep inside he felt more than a little guilt, knowing that it was his abandonment of the family which had removed his influence from his son, he was not blessed with the capability to admit this openly. As he had run his ships, with his word being unquestioned, so he expected to hold his position in the home. The emotional conflict that he now suffered lead him to paying little or no attention to his son from that time onwards.

And so it was that upon leaving school, a school where he had blended into the background so fully that none of his teachers would ever remember his name, the Visitor had found work in an Estate Agent's office. From this point office work became his life, it being an environment in which he very quickly proved himself to be adequate. His employers found him to be a person fully capable of doing exactly as he was told. He gave no cause for reprimand, nor was there ever the need to praise him for an outstanding achievement. He arrived at the office each morning on time and he left each afternoon when his day's work was done: in between he would boil a kettle when it was time to boil it, speak to buyers and vendors if they spoke to him first and put pieces of paper in their correct places. In this Estate Agent's office the first ten years of his working life, ten years in which he lost his puppy-fat to premature middle-age spread, passed with no event of note whatsoever. At the end of this time, just when it appeared that he would be content to sit at the same desk for the remaining forty years until his retirement, he suddenly developed an aversion to elastic bands.

It was not elastic bands in general that was the problem, it was his employer's elastic bands in particular. He was sat at his desk one day, idly turning one of these innocuous bits of everyday office equipment around his fingers, when a rather enlightening thought occurred to him: that the staid, 'Old family firm', dusty style of business that he worked for could be summed up by their elastic bands; basic, brown and boring. He was, after all, a young man he told himself. There was a whole world out there for him to explore, he should be making more of his life before it was too late. This dissatisfaction, he realised, had started to brew within him after watching a television documentary about a steam enthusiast. This man had travelled to many parts of the world to photograph steam engines and to record details of them that may be of interest to other steam enthusiasts. What had struck the Visitor about this programme was that the man was only the same age as himself and yet he had achieved so much! Subsequently he found himself sick and tired of the humdrum routine of life at the Estate Agents, it was beginning to stifle him. With this enlightenment came a rare moment of decision for one who had been used to accepting the world as he found it: he would go and find work in an office where they had up-to-date, coloured, elastic bands.

To this end he started answering adverts in the Situations Vacant column of the local paper: office work, any office work so long as it would take him away from the Estate Agents. Whenever he was fortunate enough to be summoned for an interview with a prospective employer his one criteria for the acceptance of a post rested on his observations of their elastic bands. It was this strategy that led him to work in tele-sales. There are some who would see this as a retrograde step while yet others may consider it a sideways move. But to the Visitor it was a giant leap forward and he threw himself into this work wholeheartedly. After a few months, however, he began to realise that his initial optimism had been misplaced. This time the issue affecting him was his decision to grow a moustache. The addition to his face of this decoration would, he reasoned, show the world that he had an adventurous spirit. Once again it had been a television programme that had planted the idea in his head, this one a documentary on the life and times of a rambler. This person was a legend amongst those of his kind: indeed, to mark the Silver Jubilee of the Queen he had walked non-stop three times around the coastline of the Isle of Wight carrying a Union Jack. This man had a moustache. As nobody else in the tele-sales office had one it suddenly seemed a good idea to the Visitor to seek a new job in an office where this, by now highly desirable, facial feature was in evidence. In a similar vein his life continued through the rest of his twenties and into his thirties. Whilst a casual observer might have seen his frequent changes of employer as mere restlessness, in the mind of the Visitor he was continually making his way in the world. Thus it was that in his mid-thirties he quite by accident found his true niche in the field of office work: Research.

It was no coincidence that this discovery coincided with the death of his parents, who passed away within weeks of each other. His mother's death had been the inevitable result of a wasting illness for which no cure was known. His father, now long retired and determined to absolve all guilt for his transgressions, nursed her tenderly to the end. Once this pitiful event had come he then saw no reason to live without her: without any fuss he had simply given up and shortly followed her into the grave. To their son this destruction of the family unit came as an unforeseen shock. He had never moved out of the family home and into a place of his own as it had never occurred to him to do so. Nor had it ever crossed his mind that one day he would have to fend for himself: due to his propensity to only make short-term decisions he was not one who was given to looking to the future at all. Ironically this was a pivotal moment for his career - such as it had been up to that point. Now, faced with personal tragedy that gave him cause to look back on his life, he became an acknowledged expert in the field of research.

It had started with his father's Merchant Navy uniform: he had been sorting through his parents belongings and had found it hanging in their wardrobe. As all talk of the sea had been absent in the home for the many years since his father's retirement it was an area of his life which, if not completely forgotten, had faded into distant memory. Its sudden reawakening via the uniform caused the Visitor, on an impulse, to try it on himself. He wanted to know how it would feel to be clothed in the rig which had been so familiar to him as a child, a rig which his recollections saw as being so much larger than what he was now seeing on the clothes hanger. The uniform would fit his frame and this realisation came as a minor shock to him. Although some twenty-five years had passed since he had last sat on his father's knee, and he had grown accordingly in the meantime, this one fact was difficult for him now to comprehend. Subsequently the actual donning of the meticulously cared for outfit was a slow process, with the mixture of guilt and awe that he experienced causing him to almost abandon the project at one point.

Once the dressing was complete however, he was pleased with how it felt against his skin. More than this, the reflection that he saw in the bedroom mirror filled him with excitement at being thus arrayed: he was a sailor, not a common sailor but a ship's Captain. He walked around the room to better get a sense of what it was to stride around the deck with the weight of command resting easily upon his shoulders. Stopping his inspection of the vessel at his mother's dressing table he picked up the framed photograph that she had always kept there, even during his father's absence. It was a picture taken of his father, grandfather and great-grandfather all in their smartest sea-faring array. All three of the men were in uniform, the peaked caps of the elder men displaying much in the way of braid. His father, still a young man, was dressed as an officer cadet. All three had the same proud bearing, the same expression of confidence. At that instant the Visitor felt himself part of their lives in a way that he had never known before and he wished that he too was in the photograph.

This in turn led him to wondering why his father had discouraged him from joining the Merchant Navy himself. At the time he had not questioned the firm prompting which had steered his mind towards other occupations but now, as he looked at the photograph, he felt a great sadness. More than this, deep inside he felt a mixture of frustration and anger: he had been denied his place in the family tradition and in this way felt he had let them down.

Replacing the picture upon the dressing table he tried recalling some of the stories he had been told as a child of the family's maritime history. But they were part of a long forgotten childhood: lost when his mother had her mind turned to unkindly thoughts towards the ways of sailors in her betrayal. Inevitably there had been an effect on her young son's impressionable mind, unintentional and subtle but no less instilled for that. Now, standing in his parents' bedroom, wearing the uniform awoke in him the desire to know everything about this family history. It was the point in his life when all his efforts, both professional and private, became directed at looking backwards. In the years that followed this became his obsession. He was desperate to be part of his family tradition and the only way he could achieve this was by researching the lives that had preceded his own. In the, somewhat random, approach that he held towards his career it naturally followed that his next job would involve research. And as a result of the fact that he started eating, breathing and sleeping for research he soon became incredibly good at it. Indeed, such was the reputation that he acquired in this area of office work, his present post had been offered to him: it was the first time in his life a new situation had sought him rather than visa versa.

Today, in the tiny room of his lodging house, he wore his father's uniform as he had done so many times since that first time some five years previously. But on this occasion it was different: hitherto it had only been worn in his own home, the house that he had inherited on the passing of his parents. There he would don it religiously whenever he was embarking upon an evening's study of old documents. These papers, which had been sought out from shipping companies all over the world, were helping him to piece together the details of a life he had never known. Ships and shipping, ports at home and abroad, coasters, deep sea vessels, crew lists, trade routes, great successes and tragic losses; all small components in the larger picture that he was wishing to comprehend. At home the uniform was a private matter but in this town, miles away from anybody who would recognise him, it would become public. He wanted to wear it out of doors: to walk along a quay and smell the fresh sea air, just as his forefathers had done. He wanted to feel, and be seen, as a ship's Captain. The image in his mind was one of a man who, although ashore, still carried the weight of responsibility for his ship and the men who crewed her: he could hold his head high and put purpose in his stride. And then after the walk he would find a place where he could enjoy some lunch. A Captain relaxing whilst he wrote up his log for the last voyage - though in reality this would be his notes on that morning's meeting with the prawnman. With this in mind he took one last admiring look at himself in the bedroom mirror and straightened his collar and tie. More than satisfied with his reflection, he picked up his notebook from the table then set out to take another small step in reclaiming his heritage.

The quay was fairly busy that day, although nowhere near as frantic as it would be two month's hence when holidaymakers would arrive in great numbers. At first, standing at the western end of the quay close to a lifting bridge, the Visitor felt a little out of place in his unfamiliar clothing. Inside he was telling himself over and over again that it was fitting that he should be dressed thus, it was his birthright. Unfortunately he had another inner voice which was making its opinion known: it was telling him that should a real ship's Captain decide to speak to him then his charade would collapse immediately. To better enable himself to ignore this second inner voice the Visitor focussed his attention on what was happening around him.

That the vessels moored alongside this end of the quay were the harbour work-boats was clear to him. His many hours spent studying the machinery of sea ports had given him the ability to identify some of these craft plus a fairly good idea as to their individual uses. The largest was plainly a tug boat, such a vessel would be recognised by even those with little knowledge of the sea. Of the others, two were the pilot cutters: this he knew simply because they had the word 'Pilots' emblazoned upon the sides of their wheelhouses. But there were also other craft whose purpose was not so obvious to him and he spent a little time in trying to guess their use. It was, he told himself eventually, one thing to read of boats and ports but to put information gained into a cohesive whole could be quite baffling. In an attempt to gain some clues to reduce this bafflement he moved closer to where the crews of these boats were going about their daily tasks. This he did in the confidence that they were intent on their painting and cleaning and would take little notice of him. As they worked they chatted amongst themselves and the Visitor strained his ears to eavesdrop, hoping for a few words that would enlighten him further. But this proved to be a futile expectation: the language they used was English but their speaking of it incorporated phrases which were incomprehensible to him. He knew that this was because they were using hybrid nautical terms and this only served to remind him that he was not a real seaman. Upon overhearing the words: "Comin' roun' Aunt Betty with four knots up me arse........." He decided it was time to walk away. One day, he told himself, I will understand. But not today.

Turning his back to the bridge he walked a short way along the quay until he stood facing a ship moored opposite. There was something familiar about this ship that had caught his attention but at first he could not think what it was. Suddenly, with heart fluttering excitement, he realised that the ship was discharging a cargo of sand. It was a sand dredger! This he knew about. He had recently discovered that his grand-father had sailed on sand dredgers for many years. By diligent research the Visitor had learned much about this trade and, as he watched, he knew exactly what was happening across the quay on the sand wharf. More, he could give a name to most of the machinery used in this operation, knew where the sand had come from and what needed to be done to it before it could be sold. He knew how many officers there were on board, how many crew and what their duties were. Of an instant he felt a lot more confident in the uniform. The sea, he told himself with great assurance, was in his blood. Reluctantly dragging his eyes away from the dredger he looked further along the wharves. One ship, he knew, did not make a sailor. He needed to see more to further test his grasp of the learning which had thus far been purely academic.

To this end, as he continued his walk, his eyes were

taking in the business of the men and machinery in a working port. On most of the wharfs opposite the Town Quay ships were loading or discharging cargoes, some of which were easily identifiable - such as timber or steel - whilst others were a mystery to him. One such was being loaded into a hold by a large dockside crane: as far as the Visitor could tell it could have been dust. The grab of the huge crane was filling itself from unidentifiable mounds piled upon the dock-side and dropping each load into the ship's hold. He stared at it for ten minutes but, try as he might, there was no way of recognising it as anything specific. Outwardly he tried to give the impression that he was viewing it all in a detached professional manner but this apparent composure served to hide an inward struggle to make sense of it all. Occasionally he made a mental note of something that needed looking into at a later date, as soon as he was at home with his books and files. But his over-riding emotion throughout was one of self-congratulation: he had found the courage to walk out in uniform and he had been rewarded for this effort by one scruffy old sand dredger. This ship had proved to him that he possessed the heart of a sailor, from that one encounter he had slipped more easily into the role that he was playing. This, he felt, was sufficient for that day: more would simply overload his mind.

So when he reached the eastern end of the quay, where the smells that reached his nostrils proclaimed it to be an area dedicated to the trade of the fisherman, he decided to sit awhile before going in search of his lunch. This was a shame really. If he had carried on walking, he would never have met Lucy Love. Without intending to she is just about to reduce our ship's Captain straight back into his more usual guise of landlubber.

Some would call it fate, others would call it jolly bad

luck: as he was sitting upon a bench, looking across the wide expense of the harbour to the hills beyond, the Visitor became aware of a woman walking towards him. Glancing in her direction, he saw a maid of about twenty years of age dressed in what could only be described as "a pretty pink frock" whilst upon her head she wore a bonnet decorated with imitation flowers, her shoes were delicate in style and in one hand she carried a little handbag and a closed parasol. In the other hand she carried a can of paraffin. Her cheeks were rosy and her lips full and red. From underneath her bonnet tumbled a mass of blonde curls. Taking all this information in with the briefest of glances two thoughts immediately struck the Visitor: that she looked ridiculously out of place on the quay and, more importantly, that he hoped she would pass quickly by. He was not entirely sure why he felt this latter quite strongly, it was not his usual reaction to strangers. Indeed, given his occupation, he would generally welcome the chance to speak to anyone. But he was just about to discover that in this hope he was to be disappointed.

The woman, intent on private thoughts of her own, remained unaware of his presence until she was almost level with where he sat. Once she did spot him her first act was to quickly hide the can of paraffin behind a nearby mooring bollard. She then allowed herself to regard him carefully as she transferred the parasol to the other hand and executed a couple of carefree swings with this accessory. Obviously satisfied with her appraisal of the Visitor she made a bee-line to the empty space next to where he was sat. In order to cover these few short steps she had exchanged the purposeful stride which had brought her thus far for shorter faster steps. Without looking at, or speaking to, him she sat down on the bench.

For a few minutes silence was all that passed between them, little was the Visitor to know that this lull could only precede a storm. In his ignorance he concentrated his gaze upon a flock of seagulls following a fishing boat into the harbour. Rather than acknowledge the woman's presence he was, rather pointlessly, attempting to count the number of birds in this flock: his hope now was that she would just go away. The woman, however, had her own ideas contrary to his and the determination to make them known. Her opening gambit was to lean the parasol against the bench beside her, leaving both hands free to open her handbag and take from within a small handkerchief. She then made a short display of dabbing at her nose with this fragrantly scented item, following which she held it out and dropped it upon the ground at the Visitor's feet.

"Oh dear," she squeaked, "I seem to have dropped something."

She then sat waiting with such expectancy that it was almost a visible entity hanging in the air between them. It was certainly more than the Visitor, brought up to ridiculously good manners, could ignore. More than a little bemused by this charade the Visitor leaned down to retrieve the wayward article from the ground. Turning to hand it back to its rightful owner he noticed, with no little shock, that his apparently youthful companion was in fact in her late forties. The loss of some twenty-five years had been achieved by the liberal use of facial make-up.

"Why, thank you kind sir."

She turned to face him, holding his gaze - a gaze that she completely failed to notice was one of horror. It was, to the Visitor, as if he had come face to face with an apparition from a nightmare. He realised that the unnaturally high pitched tone in her voice was due to the need to safeguard her cosmetics. To this end the woman spoke whilst keeping the sides of her mouth completely still, it was only the centre of her lips that moved. The overall effect was of a mannequin which, with Hollywood grotesque, had been brought to life in order to terrorise a small neighbourhood.

"Please, do not mention it." Was all he could manage by way of reply before he once again turned his attention to the flock of seagulls. Although having been thwarted in his hopes regarding this woman twice already he still had room for another hope: that this would be the end of their discourse. In this he had not counted upon the resolve of the woman to keep it going.

"Tell me," she squeaked, "if you do not think it too forward of me to ask of course. What is the name of your ship, brave Captain?"

The Visitor was taken aback by this question, having momentarily forgotten that he was wearing his father's uniform. While he sought for an answer to the enquiry the woman laid one of her scrawny, but prettily gloved, hands upon his thigh. As the realisation of how he must appear to others dawned upon him he found himself facing a moral dilemma: he simply could not voice a lie, it was not in his nature. By the same token, in this instance, nor could he tell the truth. It was too long, too complicated and too personal. Whilst his brain was engaged in trying to find a way out of this plight his mouth opened and the words; "I do not have a ship." fell out before he could stop them.

Having acted in this anarchic manner, his mouth then clamped shut again and allowed his lips to form into a sickly smile. Blind to any interpretation other than the one that she wished to apply to his words, the woman's eyes widened slightly. This was the only facial expression that she dare allow herself as evidence of her delight at his reply.

"You do not have a ship at the moment?" Her voice betrayed excitement at this notion, excitement which her body language now expressed in a series of over-dramatic postures.

"I expect your last command was shipwrecked in terrible circumstance. I can see you now, fighting the elements heroically to save the lives of your crew. The very men who previously regarded you as a tyrant, the very bane of their miserable existence, now looked to you as their saviour. And you did not fail them brave Captain, to the eternal gratitude of their wives and children. You fought against the might of nature itself and in this battle your skill was not found to be wanting."

The woman paused and her eyes changed from one reliving a grim episode in the recent past to one envisaging a rosy future.

"And now you are waiting for your new ship to be built." She spoke with a voice which trembled with anticipation.

"No doubt this means that you will be in port for weeks, perhaps months, before your new command is ready to be launched. We have this time, it is ours, a gift from Eros to two people unable to contemplate a life without each other." Her voice fell to a sad near whisper as her shoulders fell into a posture of resignation; "And then you will sail away. You will leave me forlorn upon the shore."

She lifted her head and allowed her gaze to see the distant horizons beyond the harbour entrance. Just as it seemed to the Visitor that they were doomed to remain in this stance for eternity the woman, with heart stopping swiftness, grabbed at his right hand and held it against her breast.

"But, my brave Captain," she squealed dramatically, "every single minute with you will be worth all the years of waiting! True love will always win and there is no truer love than ours! Fate has brought us together and nothing, not even the judgement day when all falls to dust, can rent us asunder!"

Not surprisingly, the Visitor's horror had by this point turned to terror. He believed the woman to be mad and himself trapped inside her madness. The act of pulling his hand towards her meant that they were now sat face to face. As their noses were within inches of each other and, as the woman was long-sighted, this caused her to suddenly go cross-eyed. Such an expression at close quarters and in the surreal circumstances could only add to the Visitor's appraisal. His mind raced as it tried to comprehend what was happening to him. Lunacy! he told himself, sheer lunacy which he had encountered in this town once before: yesterday when he met the Vicar. The linking of these two encounters then led him to wondering if the pair were related in some way. Realising that the woman now expected him to respond, he could only do so with the words;

"Do you know the local Vicar?"

At which the woman, all too ready to interpret these words as a proposal of marriage, clasped his hand tighter to her bosom.

"YES, YES, YES," she cried, forgetting to hold her face in check causing several deep ravines to appear across her countenance, "I DO, I DO, I DO."

Completely unaware that the woman now considered them to be betrothed, the Visitor could only think of escape. Such an option was made the more urgent by his terror now having turned to physical sickness at the sight of the woman's make up starting to fall off in places. The mannequin come to life was now disintegrating in front of his eyes, its hideous face cracking open as the mouth gibbered senselessly. He struggled to fight the sensation of retching in his throat as he leapt to his feet, retrieving his hand as he did so. He could not comprehend how he had become embroiled in this situation, a fact which was making his extraction from it difficult to achieve politely and politeness, he felt sure, would be his only surety against enraging the woman into a full-scale attack.

"I have to go now.....er........ Things to see, people to do........you know how it is," he stammered hurriedly and clumsily.

"Of course, my brave Captain." The woman gazed at him with the sort of eyes usually only seen on waifs portrayed in pictures for sale in some of the town's tackier art galleries. "There is so much to sort out and who knows how little time."

The Visitor could not even begin to understand what she meant by these words, nor did he wish to seek enlightenment. He just wanted to get as far away from this woman as he was able. At first he backed slowly away, alert for any sudden movement on her part. But after a few moments his fear started getting the better of him: although he knew he would be leaving himself exposed to one of her unpredictable lunges at him, he nevertheless turned and ran along the quay back to the town. His fear of further attack was, however, unfounded: the radiant figure of Lucy Love remained seated upon the bench which he had recently vacated. She was content to watch him as he retreated until out of sight. Then, sighing happily to herself, she murmured;

"He loves me, he truly truly loves me. I will go straightaway and buy him a lantern."

Chapter Six

For light entertainment Master Miles had spent half an hour standing at Fisherman's Dock. His sole purpose for being there was to watch Boathook Bald as that worthy struggled to row the sixteen foot boat across the harbour. Ordinarily this would have been no great task: to those brought up by the sea rowing a boat takes no more effort than, say, riding a bicycle. But the *Prudence* was fitted with an inboard engine which greatly increased her weight. Added to this was the awkward obstruction that it presented in the centre of the vessel, consequently she was by no means suited to propulsion by oars. To see his crewman's struggles as he attempted to keep the vessel on a course for the harbour entrance gave the Master enormous pleasure. Even at the distance of a mile Boathook Bald's face could still be seen contorting into agonising expressions with the effort: a satisfying sight to Master Miles but one which ultimately caused him to feel quite hungry. He decided to take his lunch at The Club.

The Club was an establishment officially known as 'The Ship's Captain's Reading Rooms' which was situated on the Town Quay on the first floor of a building which had originally housed the Harbour Master's office. In years gone by it had been exactly what its name suggests: a place where visiting ship's officers could relax when in port and catch up with the news. A selection of daily newspapers were provided for this very purpose and were eagerly read, and at busy times squabbled over, by those for whose benefit they were intended. But this facility had only been used fully in the days of sail, when voyages took a lot longer and the time spent in port was reckoned in days rather than hours. Seamen in those times had very little opportunity to find out what was happening beyond their own wooden walls, such was the insularity of shipboard life. It was only through such establishments as the reading rooms, found in seaports everywhere, that they could ever discover what was taking place in the rest of the world.

With the coming of motor vessels, more efficient methods of handling cargoes and better communications the reading rooms fell largely into disuse. Ships had faster turn around times with the result that Captains had less time in port. Very often a ship arriving in the morning could be discharged, loaded and then sailing again the same day with the Skipper not even having time to step ashore. Also, with the advancement of the radio age, those at sea could now hear the worldwide news transmitted to them wherever their ship happened to be. With these changing of the times the 'Ship's Captain's Reading Rooms' were no longer needed for their original design and it was at this point that the Prawning Masters took over the premises. Although their stated intention at the time was to use the rooms for the business of the Fleet it very quickly became their own exclusive club.

To this place Master Miles now made his way: it would be a good opportunity for him to catch up on the news from his fellow Masters in the Fleet. Although he had no need to hire a new crewman he had attended the Stench Fair on the previous day, this being obligatory for all the Masters and certainly expected of him as their Admiral. More than this, it was an opportunity for the Fleet as a whole to display themselves in all their finery, to show their public face to the world. But it was a strict rule that the Stench Fair was not an occasion to discuss business, it was far too public an arena for such delicate matters. For all discourse on topics that they preferred to remain in their own private domain they had The Club.

Although situated within a very short distance from Paradise, The Club boasted a far more sedate atmosphere for the Masters to relax into. It maintained its own protocol which ensured that the Masters using the facility behaved towards each other with a level of decorum which belied their professional rivalry. Any disagreements that they may have when on the Prawning Grounds, and these could be many and fiery, were temporarily forgotten within these walls. Here they took advantage of private space to indulge in unlicensed drinking and gambling behind locked doors. Indeed, a Prawning Master who wished to spend a day or a night in convivial company would find all he wished for with no fear of interruption, it was the heart of their empire. And as the rooms looked out upon the part of the quay where the Stench Fair was held this gave the Masters the feeling of being 'Kings of all that they surveyed'. Whatever was happening along the rest of the Town Quay, this area was theirs and was acknowledged as such by the local community. In this small way the original intention of establishing themselves as an elite had succeeded: though they may have to go to the Fisherman's Dock to work, the image that the town held of the Masters was firmly rooted in their being smartly attired and walking into The Club.

All of the catering arrangements required by the Masters were overseen by a formidable woman in her late fifties known, affectionately, as Sweaty Betty. She was content to let the Prawning Masters act as Monarchs safe in the knowledge that she was the Queen who ruled this small Kingdom. Although Betty never had the need to assert this authority there were few men who would contradict her if she ever did, such was her utmost confidence in the belief that the availability of good food outweighed any other consideration in life.

Food had been her own life: not with the eyes of the glutton but with the passion of an artist. Upon leaving school she had joined her family's business, which was conducted from the kitchen of their end of terrace house close to the Fisherman's Dock. This small concern had been started by her grandparents and was a perfect example of that generation's dislike of waste.

Knowing that a certain percentage of the fish landed at the port was unsaleable, usually due to low demand for a particular species, they would buy up this surplus at a reasonable cost. From these fish they would then produce all manner of pies and delicacies blending the basic ingredient with herbs which, if not grown in their own garden, could be found in hedgerows not far from the town. The result of their labours found a ready market in the local restaurants and fishmongers.

Their products soon earned them a good reputation for taste and texture, at a cost to suit the most strict of household budgets. They made no secret of this success: it was all down to the recipes that had been in local families for generations, a by-product of having to feed large broods from a shallow purse. With this simple approach the business thrived, so much so that Betty's parents inherited a comfortable living when they in turn became its owners. A further increase in their trade came about by Betty's own speciality - fishcakes. When she started taking an active role in the preparation of these items it soon became clear that her creations were unique for she had that certain touch which would transform this humble dish into a rare delicacy. They were to be the making and, sadly, the breaking of a golden era for this family firm.

As these opportunities are wont to do, a sudden uplift in their fortunes came about quite by chance. The buyer for a noted London store had been staying with relatives in one of the town's suburbs. During this visit he had been served a meal which included Betty's fishcakes and was so impressed that he requested to know their origin. A few further enquiries led him to arranging a meeting with Betty's parents for the purpose of a business proposition;

"These fishcakes will sell in London." he told them.

"How many a week can you supply me with?" he had asked.

With a few reservations, not being the sort of people who would easily be impressed by talk of the capital, they promised to phone him in the not too distant future. To these down to earth folk the reaction of Betty herself to the idea carried a lot more weight than fancy words from a man in a suit: she alone would be the one to say whether or not the scheme was viable. To this end a family meeting was held at which the production of fishcakes was discussed at length.

Upon one thing all three were agreed: that this opportunity to extend their business was not to be to the detriment of their local trade. The vast majority of their customers were also acquaintances, people whose businesses had grown with their own. There was a great sense of loyalty involved and no amount of enticement from London would be more important than this: money could not buy such friendship. But, with the pound signs nevertheless rolling in front of their eyes, they were also keen to find a way to take advantage of this opening.

There would be, in Betty's view, only one problem to overcome with the necessary increase in production. It was not in the blending of the ingredients to her special recipe, nor in the mixing which had to be just right to keep the texture. These stages in the process could be scaled up with very little trouble. But the final task of hand moulding each fishcake to the perfect shape and size would be time consuming on a larger scale. And this was the part of the enterprise that she insisted she could entrust to no other, she firmly maintained that this simple process, if not performed correctly, would be the ruin of the whole venture. She also announced that she was determined to find a solution to this problem.

And with a great amount of thought, practice and perseverance she eventually succeeded. Previously she had spent thirty seconds in scooping four ounces of the mixture out of the bowl and shaping it upon the table. Now she had found a way whereby she took just five seconds for each one. Getting the weight right was easy: after many years spent at this work picking up exactly the right amount had become second nature to her. For the pressing and shaping process she stood before the table stripped to the waist. The bowl of mixture would be placed to her right. Then as she scooped up a portion of the concoction in her right hand she would raise her left arm to shoulder level. In one swift movement she would place the right hand with its contents into her left armpit and, by allowing her left arm to drop, squeeze the mixture into a perfectly shaped fishcake. This she would then place on the table as part of one single fluid movement of her right hand as it travelled back to the bowl. Time after time this process was repeated: it was a wonderful example of the human body's powers of coordination and to an onlooker it would have appeared as if Betty was conjuring fishcakes out of thin air. So it was that the noted London store was supplied with as many fishcakes as it wanted without the local outlets being deprived of their best selling commodity.

For a few years the family prospered, the name that they had made for themselves with Betty's speciality having a positive effect on the sales of their other products. Another business, finding itself in a similar fortunate position, might well have considered moving their operations to larger premises. Not so with Betty's family. They were making far more money than they had ever thought possible but money, in their opinion, existed for one purpose only: once the essential household expenses had been met the residue was directed towards leading a riotous social life. As the town boasted many lively inns which the local folk would frequent and drink to whatever excess their purse allowed, they did not have to look far for the simple pleasures in life. To Betty's family more spare cash meant that their excesses could be more extreme, they worked hard and they played even harder. Their barometer for a good night out was measured in the number of bruises that they woke up with the following morning, for who can enjoy themselves to the full without sustaining the occasional minor personal injury? But any such injuries would be immediately forgotten once they set their minds to the day's work to be done. These years, for Betty, were idyllic.

Unfortunately, but inevitably, their use of the family home for business purposes came to the attention of the Town Corporation. This body of well-to-do townsfolk found it contrary to all the natural order of society to see such ordinary people doing so well for themselves: though none could say precisely why, it felt as if a law was being broken. At one of their regular meetings they discussed the problem and agreed that such enterprise must be stamped out before others tried to emulate their initiative, for to allow it to continue could well lead to anarchy. It was no coincidence that the member most indignant at this state of affairs, and who had instigated the debate, had plans to open a food factory on the edge of the town himself. Needless to say, he wished to include fishcakes on his assembly lines and it was he who suggested to the Corporation that their first line of attack should be the sending in of Public Health Inspectors. Inwardly he then experienced a small moment of triumph when this motion was accepted unanimously: though a small family concern could never hope to compete against the scale of production that he envisaged for his own factory, his envious nature felt no small degree of pain in knowing of their good reputation. This was something that he coveted for himself and since boyhood he had been used to getting his own way.

He it was who made it his own business to see this decision put into action without delay and the very next day the Inspectors paid an unannounced visit to their unwitting victims. As their arrival coincided with Betty being in full production mode the Town Corporation had no need of a second line of attack. The Public Health Inspectors, referred to by Betty's family as "Them nosey bastards in white coats and gas masks", subsequently brought a successful prosecution upon the business. It was closed down overnight and, due to the costs incurred, its bank balance depleted to the point that they were ruined.

There was extensive publicity surrounding the case which caused varied public reaction. The newspapers made much of the information that a semi-naked woman was found to be engaged in the production of fishcakes. By careful use of words they managed to convey the idea that there was something sexual in this. Once this slant was taken up by the cartoonists who contributed to the tabloids it was reinforced and within a week of the story first breaking it had entered the national psyche as accepted fact: everybody who lived in Betty's part of the country used fishcakes in their sex lives. The news reports had also noted that several cats were found to be wandering around the food preparation area. Subsequently the phrase "fishcakes and pussies" was one guaranteed to raise a laugh if used by a comedian.

In Betty's neighbourhood the reaction was one of outrage against the Corporation and the newspaper reporters. They discovered that their words, innocently spoken to journalists in efforts to defend the family, had been printed out of context and completely at odds with their true meaning. A photograph of Betty walking into a local bakery shop appeared in many of the tabloids. This shot accompanied a fabricated story claiming that she spent hundreds of pounds a week on cat food. The neighbours were angry to discover that innocent folk, honest hard working people, could be persecuted in this way. As for the cats: of course there were cats! How else was the family supposed to keep the rats and the mice away? As they were aware of the truth, those who lived in the immediate vicinity strongly supported Betty and her family.

Slightly further afield in the suburbs of the town genteel folk tutted and frowned at the behaviour of the lower classes. They would deny to each other that they had ever bought any of the family's products. This, they claimed, was because they had "Always known that something was going on," and that they had "Been totally convinced that one day this sort of thing would happen". Needless to say, such sanctimonious utterings only began after they had relocated their own plentiful supply of Betty's fishcakes from the freezer to the dustbin - triple wrapped so that the binmen would not notice what was amongst their rubbish.

The member of the Town Corporation who intended to open the food factory acted swiftly. Seeing an opportunity to link his name with matters of hygiene he made an immediate and public donation to the church funds. In this way he ensured that the Vicar's next sermon was on the subject of "Cleanliness is next to Godliness". There was also a strong emphasis on the fact that there was a 'right' way to do things and a 'wrong' way. Certain events in the town had shown that it was God's will that nowadays food should be prepared in modern factories.

The noted London store issued a press statement: It was with regret that they had discovered that some of the products on their shelves had failed to meet their own, very strict, standards. Whilst they wished to assure any of their valued patrons who had purchased these items that they were in no danger, the store would cease retailing certain products forthwith. Patrons who had items purchased from the store who wished to return them were guaranteed a full refund. This decision had been taken by the board purely on the grounds of customer service. The noted London store did not make it publicly known that their head buyer had tended his resignation.

The end result of the affair for Betty herself was that she was unemployed and, it seemed, unemployable. The only skill that she had developed, other than the production of fishcakes, was as a champion arm wrestler. Whilst this ability could reap its rewards in wagers when unsuspecting visiting sailors were in town it could by no means be counted upon as a regular source of income. It was at this point that one of her uncles, who also happened to be a Prawning Master, took pity on her plight and he suggested to his fellow

Masters that she would be a suitable candidate for a recently vacated post at The Club. The job description for this was somewhat flexible - never was the term 'Head Cook and Chief Bottle-washer' more apt. But the pay was above average and the working conditions were relaxed and easy for the right applicant. When Betty was called before the Admiral of the Prawning Fleet for an interview it immediately became clear that the job would suit her and that she would suit the job. She was given the post with only one stipulation: if she removed any of her clothing whilst cooking the agreement would be terminated. This one reference to her recent upheaval, made in jest, was the only time that the topic was referred to: Betty's willingness to work hard and her cheerful personality soon endeared her to the Prawning Masters, to the point that her unfortunate persecutions were soon forgotten by all. For Betty it gave the opportunity to deal with life's tribulations in the only way that she knew how: by rolling up her sleeves and getting on with some honest work.

~~*~~

Arriving at The Club Master Miles poked his head around the door of the kitchen to enquire of the menu that day. Upon receiving Sweaty Betty's reply, along with her recommendation, he ordered his dish and then made his way into the main room: it was here that the Prawning Masters gathered to eat, drink and to socialise in each other's company. This large high-ceilinged room, by its very existence, epitomised everything that they stood for and lived for. Its decoration and furnishings were the very embodiment of how they viewed themselves and their standing in the community.

The south facing wall was the only one in the room which had windows set into it. There were four of these, large areas of glass which created a bright airy atmosphere within. The remaining three walls featured a number of framed works of art which served to break up the monotony of bare walls. It might be supposed that being men of the sea these would be of nautical scenes, but this was not so. The Masters in the Prawning Fleet held the opinion that their Club was a place to occasionally escape from thoughts of their work rather than indulge in them. That they were men who preferred to keep their lives simple was reflected the choice of art: black and white depictions of classical scenes which were easy on the eye and yet cleverly detailed when studied closely. Far more important to them than these randomly purchased paintings were the furnishings that the room boasted.

Half of the room, covering the floorspace closest to the windows, was taken up with the Masters' long dining table. Of solid oak with matching chairs it was here that they would sit to share a meal, to discuss important matters pertaining to the Fleet or to gamble at the cards. Around the rest of the room were placed the individual Masters' personal armchairs. These they provided for themselves to suit their own comfort and by the side of each one stood a small table. Upon this a Master could place a glass of his favourite tipple and, if desired, an ashtray or pipe-stand. Against the three walls displaying the artwork stood the drinks lockers, each Master owning and stocking one of these magnificent cabinets. This procession of polished mahogany was broken only by the door and the ornate fireplaces situated at either end of the room. Overall these furnishings stood as a monument to the Prawning Masters generosity to their own creature comforts. Above the fireplace set into the eastern wall hung a large mirror: it was to this that the Admiral's eyes were automatically drawn upon entering the room. More than satisfied with his reflection he then turned to see who else was using The Club that day. With a mixture of surprise and delight he discovered that the only other occupant of the room was a tall elderly man who he had not seen for many years.

"Chick! Chick Bateman!" exclaimed Master Miles walking towards the man stood looking out of a window, "What brings you here?"

"Came over for a family funeral of course. Nothing else ever brings me back these days. Or, if you are asking what I am doing in The Club, I'm waiting for one of you buggers to walk in and offer me a drink. A proper drink that is, they only had bloody sherry at the send off!" replied Chick Bateman, Master (Retired) of the local Prawning Fleet. He turned to extend a hand of welcome to his younger colleague, a gesture which was eagerly reciprocated by the Admiral. As he did so he noted with amusement that the older man had yet again increased the level of Englishness in his dress and speech: having sold his home and boat some years previously in order to join in the exodus of his fellow countrymen buying cheap properties in France, Chick Bateman had displayed a growing tendency to play the Englishman abroad. At first this had manifested itself as a conscious piece of play-acting as an amusement to his friends, born out of an excitement to be making such a move to foreign climes. But as the years passed it had become so absorbed into his persona that he now carried this caricature of The Empire as if he was born to it.

"But of course," said Master Miles, "it will be very fine to share Port with you - I presume it is still Port?"

On receiving the affirmative to his question Master Miles made his way over to one of the cabinets, returning with a bottle of Port and two glasses. As he passed the door which led to the kitchen he called through to Sweaty Betty, asking her to double up on his food order.

"I've no doubt you are waiting for somebody to feed you as well," he commented as he motioned towards the dining table by way of invitation, "so I've taken the liberty of ordering for you. How is France?"

"Bloody wonderful!" The reply came firmly and without hesitation as the two men took their seats. "Except it's full of Frenchies. Best thing I ever did, moving over there. Got a cheap house, still get out in the boat sometimes, nothing serious of course, and make a few shillings here and there to top up the coffers. Wanted to get down here yesterday for the fair but had this old aunty to bury. How did it go? Who have you got this year?"

"I've got Boathook Bald again. It could be worse." admitted Master Miles.

"Your family have been using the Balds for years," the ex-prawnman shot the other a piercing look. "What is it? Have they got something on you? It's always been the tradition in the Fleet to change the crewman regularly. It stops them from getting too comfortable."

The younger man uncorked the bottle of Port, the finest that money could buy, and filled up the two glasses. Handing one across the table to its grateful recipient he decided that it was time to come clean about a closely-held family secret. Chick Bateman had long been his friend: indeed, when Master Miles had reached an age where he could join the Fleet it was Chick who had been his mentor, always ready to pass on the benefit of his experience to him. He had also proved himself to be a discreet confidante on the occasions when an older man's advice was sought.

Nevertheless, it was with a little hesitation that Master

Miles approached a subject which could prove highly embarrassing;

"I don't suppose you remember my great-grandfather, always referred to as 'Old Master Miles?'"

"No, not really. I remember seeing him around the Dock when I was a child, but it's only a vague memory. I was only a toddler myself. Of course, as I grew up, I used to hear many tales about him. It was he who single-handedly saved the Prawning Fleet from oblivion, wasn't it. He was certainly spoken of with respect amongst my elders. You must be very proud to be of his blood!"

"Well, yes, of course," Master Miles glanced out of a window, slightly embarrassed by what he had to say next. But, having made up his mind to speak on the subject, he took a deep breath and continued, "but there is one story about him that the family don't really talk about. I only found out about it myself through overhearing small snippets when my parents didn't know I was listening. When I was older I did get told the full facts, but only to serve as a warning to me: that even the greatest reputation could be destroyed by one foolish act. I shall tell you about it, this much you deserve for the sound friendship you have always shown me. It seems that in the years just after the Great War the prawning went into a decline. They certainly didn't catch the sort of numbers to maintain a fleet and boats were being pulled up on the hard and left there to rot. Masters were giving up on the prawns and looking elsewhere to earn a living. But not Old Master Miles. He was determined to stay here and keep the fishery going and, more importantly, keep the traditions alive. Which, to his credit, he did. And throughout those years the only man willing to crew for him was the Old Bald, my present man's great-grandfather, all the rest had also moved on to other work.

So they went out season after season, working the pots for all they were worth with never much to show for it. What we nowadays would call an extremely lean year they would have seen as a very good year. It was, by all accounts, a terrible time which, without great-grandfathers efforts, would have been the death knell of the Fleet. But it was worth it."

The two men sat in silence for a while, staring out of the window at a hard ebb tide carrying various bits of flotsam down between the quays. Eventually, with a sigh, Master Miles once again continued with his tale;

"Yes, it was worth it. Things started to pick up again and the prawns came back in greater numbers. Old Master Miles was vindicated in the eyes of those who had thought him a fool to suffer for the sake of the traditions. Now, suddenly, he was the hero of the hour and Masters flocked back to the fishery. The trouble was that by this time the Old Bald was knackered - no work left in him whatsoever."

"I should jolly well think so too," observed the retired Master, "they don't last forever, those crewmen. So I suppose he was told to clear off out of it and make way for a younger chap."

"Well, that is the strange part of the whole affair." said Master Miles, his voice betraying genuine bafflement, "Perhaps the years of worry had made great-grandfather's brain go soft, there was also a theory that he may have taken a bang on the head somehow. Whatever the reason, we do know that he took leave of his senses. He looked at the Old Bald and felt sorry for him."

"Goodness gracious me!" Chick Bateman sat bolt upright in his seat, scarcely able to believe his ears, "Why on earth would he want to go and do a thing like that?"

"The secret died with him I'm afraid." Master Miles looked

sad, "What we do know is that he was heard ranting on about 'Poor Old Bald' and how he'd come to the end of his working life with nothing to show for it, nothing to see him through his last years and that he was not going to let this happen. The next thing that anybody knew was that he had gone round to the old fellow's house, pulled out a pistol and shot him."

"What?! Such behaviour is plain madness!" Chick Bateman was stunned at this twist in the story, "Bullets cost good money! Why didn't he just tie a rock around the old boy's neck and chuck him into the quay?"

"Who can say? Great-grandfather obviously wasn't thinking straight."

"Well, I can certainly understand why your family have kept this a secret. If this became common knowledge, goodness me, all of the crewmen would be expecting provision to be made for their old age!"

"To get back to your original question Chick. Ever since this wayward act of kindness by Old Master Miles, the Balds' have been willing to go out of their way to work for my family. We cannot seem to get rid of them. It does have its upside though - they do work hard and long, plus they expect little in the way of payment."

Further discourse on this painful subject was temporarily halted by the arrival at the table of their lunch: warming plates of beef stew borne in the hands of Sweaty Betty. Such was her skill at improving upon standard recipes that the aroma which assailed the two men's nostrils greatly increased their appetite. They each attacked the meal with a will, accompanied by a silence that only comes with extremely good food. The resulting peace lasted until they had consumed the substance of the dish and were reduced to chasing the stock around their plates with the cutlery.

Chick Bateman was the first to speak:

"Thank you young man, I enjoyed that. And thank you also for telling me about your great-grandfather. I can quite understand why your family keep it to themselves. A most unfortunate episode, we will leave it where it is. Now, how about bringing me up to date on the local news. Did I hear a whisper that the *'Little Lady'* was lost?"

"Sunk to the bottom and good riddance!" Master Miles spoke these words with great feeling, "We don't see Master Emery in here any more, he's bought himself a cup."

"It's his own fault, whatever the circumstances. He was a disgrace to the Fleet!" Declared Chick Bateman, "I always said that one day his comeuppance would come up."

Master Peter Emery of the Prawning Vessel '*Little Lady*' had indeed bought himself a cup - an expression meaning that he had fallen in the eyes of his peers. So low was this fall that, instead of drinking from a cut-crystal glass in The Club, he now drank from a china cider cup in Paradise. And, it was true, there was nobody but himself to blame for the drop in his social standing.

His boat had earned the nickname *'Poison Dwarf'* among the crewmen. At twelve foot long she was too small for the task of prawning as it gave a very cramped space to work in. Badly maintained, she leaked constantly and required constant baling out, this effort greatly increasing the workload of the crewman. To cap it all, Master Emery was cursed with a foul and unpredictable temper and, as a result, none of them would accept a seasons work with him. To the utter disgust of the other Masters in the Fleet this meant that he had to do all of the manual work himself. They found it extremely embarrassing to witness this self degradation in one who was expected to always keep his hands clean.

There were times, however, that working single-handed was

not possible. When the wind changed from the prevailing south westerlies to a stiff easterly blow two hands were needed to work the boat, the Master taking the helm and devoting all of his attention to keeping his vessel clear of danger whilst the crewman would be stood at the bow to give warning of hidden rocks. Working as a team they would retrieve the pots as the heavy seas built up over the prawning grounds. At times such as these Master Emery had no option other than using the services of the Lipton boys in their capacity as boarders to supply him with the all important second hand. These had been the circumstances the previous October: not only were easterlies forecast, the prediction was for these winds to reach gale force. If his pots were not brought ashore they could be scattered and lost as nature threw its might in their direction: this would be an expensive catastrophe for any Prawning Master. The Lipton boys, hurriedly contacted, assured Pete Emery that he would have a crewman at dawn the following day. So it was that, as the inns were ringing their bells to announce the close of business that night, the brothers set out to scour the streets around the quay. They would ensure that their part of the agreement would be met.

Now, it just so happened that a representative of the Russian ladies shot-putting team had been visiting the town that day. For the sake of convenience we will refer to her as Mila. Upon her arrival that afternoon Mila had booked into a hotel, partaken of an early evening meal and then set off to take a short walk nearby. She felt the need for fresh air to unwind from the long hours she had spent on buses and trains that day for, being an athlete, such inactivity took its toll upon both her mind and body. And unwind she did, beyond all of her expectations: whilst walking along the Town Quay she espied a Russian ship moored against one of the wharves opposite. This awoke in her the age old need of a foreigner in a strange land to make contact with those who spoke the same language. Having been out of her own country for a fortnight by this time, Mila was wearying of conversations that involved much misunderstanding and having to repeat herself constantly. To find her way around the quays to this ship would be easy and, she felt, the effort rewarding. Thus it was that twenty minutes later she was being warmly welcomed aboard by the Captain, one Vladimir by name.

Mila then proceeded to spend the rest of the evening with the Captain and his officers in talk and, as the hours wore on, songs of their homeland far away. As they did so they toasted everything and anything they could think of with shots of Vodka, of which Vladimir seemed to have an endless supply. In Russia Mila was a renowned athlete and a national celebrity due to the amount of Olympic gold medals that she had gained to the glory of her country. To be in the presence of such exalted company was something of an occasion for the ship's crew, that her arrival at the top of their gangway was an unexpected surprise made them feel honoured indeed. It was to the regret of all parties when the time eventually came for Mila to take her leave, friendships which had been formed during impromptu merrymaking being the hardest to forgo. It was after the exchange of many hugs and mutual expressions of gratitude that Mila, politely declining the offer of an escort back to the hotel, set off to retrace her footsteps back through the town. Whereupon she soon became hopelessly lost.

A combination of the darkness in the narrow streets, which she had last seen in the evening light, and the amount of Vodka she had drunk now left her confused about her route. At first she was not too worried. She knew that the town was small and she was therefore confident about eventually reaching her destination. Another consideration was her sobriety: the act of walking thus far made her aware of exactly how much of her nation's spirit she had imbibed. There could be a benefit gained from allowing herself to sober up a little before arriving back at her hotel. She was, after all, a guest in this country and an ambassador for her own and did not wish to do either an injustice. However, after an hour of aimless wandering she began to feel more than a little frustrated at her plight. Every street that she took away from the quay, after making a few turns into lanes that she was sure she recognised, always brought her back to where she had started from. The town, it appeared, was a maze in which the stranger would have no chance of escaping from without the advice of one who knew its secrets. She was therefore pleased that she had taken the precaution of writing the name of her hotel on a piece of paper which she had in her pocket, experience of foreign travel having taught her that this was good practice. She decided to show this to the next person that she encountered in the hope that they would understand her need for directions, her command of the English language not being adequate enough to ask this question. Almost as soon as she had made this decision she turned a corner and met the Lipton boys.

But the three brothers did not recognise the sight that confronted them as being a lost female Russian athlete: they saw a sailorman slightly unsteady on his feet who would be the ideal target for their night's enterprise. Their mistake was quite understandable: Mila was by no means a great beauty, nor even a minor one, and was possessed of a physique that many body-builders only attained through the use of steroid tablets. Being well practised in their work the brothers did not need to discuss tactics amongst themselves. As Mila approached them proffering her piece of paper two of the brothers made a pretence of studying it. As they did so the third quickly moved into a position that enabled him to deliver a swift blow to the back of the sailorman's head with a cosh. From then on their work was easy. While two of them manhandled their victim back to their boarding house, the third went ahead to ensure that the local constable was not around to interfere with their business. Once safely behind the closed doors of this establishment the three took time to inspect their investment: A good strong man, on this they were all agreed, they had done well. When the hapless Mila began to show signs of recovering from the blow, the Liptons coaxed a drink between her lips. This was brandy blended with just enough knock-out drops to ensure deep sleep for the next twelve hours. In the resulting stupor, unceremoniously conveyed in a wheelbarrow, she was delivered to Master Emery of the Prawning Vessel *'Little Lady'* at dawn the following day.

Later that morning, drifting across the Prawning Grounds, Master Emery was waiting for his new crewman to show signs of life. When he did so it would be made clear to him that he was here to work, with good grace or without it making no difference to the Master. Once the work was complete the crewman would be returned to the shore: if he had accepted his shanghaiing with no sign of mutinous discontent he may even be rewarded with the price of a meal. But only one and a cheap one at that, the Lipton boys were the main recipients of such a crewman's share of the day's profits. The best a common sailor could hope for in this circumstance was a quick end to the day's labour. If, once ashore, he tried to lay a complaint against the perpetrators who had profited from the criminal act which had put him into such slavery he would lose the case: there was no proof of guilt to back up the claim, the Master would testify that the man had been an agitator who hoped to profit from such a charge. It was the word of one man against another. More than this, the sailors knew better than to anger the boarders: retribution would be swift and far more damaging than the indignity that had already been suffered. People such as the Liptons were beyond the law, not for them the niceties of the statute book whilst they had the option of ruling by fear.

It was towards the hour of noon when Mila started showing signs of coming to. Her eyes began attempts at opening and these first indications of wakefulness were followed by her endeavouring to stand. Master Peter Emery, as was his wont, threw a bucket of cold seawater in her direction to further speed the process. This first encouragement had the effect of stopping her unfocused eyes from rotating slowly in their sockets. As she sat up, however, Mila transfixed Master Emery with a stare which made him think twice about letting forth with the mouthful of abuse that he had prepared for her full awakening. Somewhere within his brain he felt the first twinges of fear: there was something dreadful in that stare.

To explain fully the nature of this something would require the expertise of a neurologist. One fully acquainted with the various toxins which had been introduced into Mila's body since the previous evening and their subsequent effect upon the nerve centres of the brain. This would have led our neurologist to the following conclusions: Firstly, that the knock-out drops had given her a headache. The sort of headache which adversely affects the temper of the sufferer, to the point that the only social interaction that they are capable of is one of extreme violence. This is commonly known as 'a bear with a sore head'. Secondly, the alcohol had greatly increased her libido to the extent that only immediate satisfaction would suffice. This is commonly known as 'gagging for it'.

Being in a twelve foot boat, three miles from the nearest piece of land, meant that it was only the prawnman upon whom Mila could give vent to these two overpowering emotions. Master Peter Emery of the *'Little Lady'*, with nowhere to hide, really should have thrown himself overboard at this point. Instead, like a rabbit caught in the glare of a car's headlights, he remained rooted to the spot as his new crewman rose to his feet. Still holding his gaze Mila slowly removed all of her clothes: as she did so the terrible realisation of what the look meant became clear to the Master, even without a neurologist on hand to explain it. As a male sailor became a female shot-putter in front of his eyes her look conveyed lust, hatred and determination all in equal quantities. Once naked and before closing in on her prey she flexed her powerful biceps: in this one single movement she showed, and he comprehended, that resistance was futile. Aboard the *'Little Lady'* there then occurred a coital storm, the ferocity of which her badly maintained timbers were unable to withstand.

Once her libidinous appetite was satiated Mila discovered her mood somewhat improved. She no longer felt any anger towards the beau who had given such gratification: this despite the fact that he was a reluctant partner who had visibly flinched each time she had demanded more. Finding herself treading water, surrounded by wreckage that was until recently a Prawning vessel, she decided that she had seen enough of England. With this decision came instant action and she turned her back and swam away from it. After sixty-eight miles of steady progress southwards she finally walked ashore in France, here she was hurriedly clothed, fed and eventually repatriated to her homeland with the minimum of diplomatic embarrassment.

As for Pete Emery, he too swam. For the former Master of the *'Little Lady'* the distance to be covered was a good deal less, the closest shore being within easy reach. From here he made his way back to the town a changed man: changed not only in his status but also by virtue of the fact that he had lost the power of coherent speech. This loss lasted for a period of three weeks, during which he could only communicate with the sort of sounds that chimpanzees emit. By the time he came to remember how to speak nobody cared enough to ask him what had happened to his boat. Nor, for shame, did he have any inclination to tell anyone: an inner voice had long been warning him that he should mend his ways before it was too late. Thus, it was a wiser and sadder man who walked into Paradise and bought himself a cup.

Chapter Seven

The Visitor woke from a deep restful sleep and immediately wondered why he had not suffered from any nightmares: he usually did when he was away from home. His next thought concerned the woman on the quay. After making his escape from Lucy Love the previous day he had returned straightaway to his lodgings, all thoughts of lunch abandoned as he sought refuge behind locked doors. Inside the safety of his room he allowed himself a few moments of deep breathing for relaxation: it was at this point that he realised he was shaking uncontrollably, so effected had he been by his encounter with Lucy Love. To aid the process of calming himself he closed his eyes and concentrated on thoughts of the sand dredger at the quay. It did not work, he could not rid his mind of the woman's image. Opening his eyes again his first thought was that the curtains were open and, in a panic, he leapt across to close them. Almost as soon as he had done this, however, a new fear gripped him: that when he opened them he would see her face peering in at him. The fact that his room was on the first floor of the building did not, in his illogical frame of mind, discount this possibility. Unable to cope with these irrational fears, he then decided that he needed to busy himself with matters more akin to his everyday existence: to this end he changed out of his father's uniform and into his more usual clothes. As a matter of course he would have then packed the uniform back into its traveling cover, but instead he hung it from the picture rail that ran around the walls of his room. He wanted to be able to admire it as he wrote up his notes on his meeting with the prawnman, a task to which he knew he must now set his mind.

Normally this part of his job would take him very little time as experience had given him the skill to pick out the areas which he recognised as marketable. But on this occasion two things were making it difficult for him to apply himself to the task. Firstly there was the information with which he had to form a coherent picture, the essence of these peoples lives. It had a certain unreality to it which became more marked when out of the company of his informant. Not that he disbelieved what he had been told, indeed, he had no need to doubt the prawnman whatsoever. In the enthusiasm with which he had shown in sharing his knowledge on matters concerning the Prawning community the man had no lack of sincerity. But the Visitor was finding that each piece of data related to another in such a way that it was impossible to separate them: nothing made sense without knowing something else. The company that he worked for only dealt in the merest snippets of information, images that were intended for a public with a very limited attention span. The second distraction, which was preventing the Visitor from being able to devote himself fully to the job in hand, were the parting words of the woman on the quay: *'There is so much to sort out and who knows how little time?'* All to often his concentration would wander from his notebook as he pondered on what these words might mean. He could make no sense of them whatsoever but, uncomfortably, something was telling him that they had great significance. The more he thought about this the more he realised that he was getting nowhere: he should put this woman out of his mind or he would get one of his headaches. But, try as he might, he was unable to do so and not even the occasional admiring glance at the uniform would bring him the hoped for comfort. The whole scenario was the perfect breeding ground for one of his nightmares. Why, he now asked himself, had it not happened?

His waking reverie was broken by someone tapping gently on his bedroom door. Before he had a chance to inquire of the reason for this he heard the apologetic voice of his landlady;

"Terribly sorry, but you do have to be downstairs by eight o'clock if you want breakfast."

"Don't worry Mrs Cousins," the Visitor replied as he stretched his body under the bedclothes to savour the warmth and cosiness within, "I will be down by then."

"Terribly sorry," the landlady's tone was even more apologetic than previously, "but it is half past eight. You have missed breakfast and I do need to get into your room now and change the bedding. It's Wednesday."

Half past eight! The Visitor sat bolt upright in the bed and looked at his travelling alarm clock. How he hated that clock, he hated all alarm clocks! He considered them one of life's evils - a necessary evil perhaps but an evil nevertheless. In all of his working years he had never come to terms with the need to be woken up each morning by such an uncouth object. Worse, when he forgot to set the alarm, as he had done the night before, it failed to wake him up altogether. This, illogically but naturally, sent him to greater heights of loathing. In a moment of unreasonable fury he wanted to throw the alarm clock against the wall: he wanted to hear it smash and then see it laying in pieces upon the bedroom floor. Instead of doing this, however, he sheepishly called out to Mrs Cousins to say that he would vacate the room shortly. He then hurriedly dressed after splashing cold water upon his face from the small washbasin which stood in the corner.

Half past eight! He realised that he would have to move quickly or he would be late for that morning's meeting with Boathook Bald. In the usual manner of one attempting to leave home in a hurry he had to try more than once to get out of the house. Each time he reached the front door he would then discover that he had left something behind in his room: first it was his notebook, then it was his shoes that sent him running back up the stairs. Lastly it was his wallet, for which he searched the room in growing panic before discovering that it had been in his pocket all along. But at long last he was finally ready to set off for the Town Cellars where, arriving breathless ten minutes later than the arranged time, the Visitor embarked upon an apology for his lack of punctuality. But with a dismissive wave of his hand the prawnman halted him in mid-sentence;

"That's a'right. We got a sayin' down 'ere that goes 'There aint no point in rushin' through life, there's only death at the end of it!' Now then, get y'breath back an' then, when y'got me drink sorted, I'll tell y'some more of our traditions."

Red-faced with the exertions that he had undergone since his failure to smash the alarm clock, the Visitor sat down heavily next to Boathook Bald.

"I suppose you will need another bottle of rum?"

"No, not rum t'day ta. I fancies some cider t'day. You'll 'ave t'get it from Leggy down there," Boathook Bald pointed in the direction of Paradise some twenty yards away, "See where that dog is sat?"

The Visitor looked to where a flea bitten hound of unfathomable lineage was attempting to lick its own nether regions, an act which was causing it to rotate slowly upon the pavement where it sat. As there was no other dog in sight the Visitor nodded to indicate that, so far, he fully understood the instructions.

"Well," continued the prawnman, "Right by that dog is a door. Y'go in that door and see Leggy, but y'got t'remember that y'dressed smart. So y'got t'be quick about tellin' 'im what y'want an' that it's f'r me. Otherwise 'e might think y'from the Corp'ration an' then 'e'll beat you up y'see."

Struggling to his feet the Visitor cautiously walked towards the door by the dog. He was halfway there when the prawnman, struck by a sudden thought, called out to him;

"Tell Leggy I'll 'ave a 'God–f'rgive-me'. It'll save on y'legs!"

Upon reaching the door the Visitor hesitated: never had going to fetch a drink carried with it such a threat to his personal safety. But he need not have worried, from the other side of the door a voice shouted;

"Well come in then, if you're bastard well coming in!"

At this obvious invitation, and more than a little relieved that somebody from within had issued it, he pushed open the door and entered Paradise. Inside the light was almost non-existent and he had to hesitate again whilst his eyes adjusted to the gloom. Just as he was feeling confident enough to move forward without falling over the furniture packed tightly into a space barely large enough to contain it, the voice spoke to him again;

"Don't worry, I aint going to bastard well eat you!"

By now, with the direction of the voice to focus upon, the Visitor could discern the body to which it belonged. Across the large room in which he found himself standing a man was busying himself behind a bar. The Visitor felt that at this point he should state his mission.

"I've......er......"

"Don't worry, I know why you're bastard well here." the man interrupted him, "I heard that old bastard shouting at you. I reckon the whole bastard town must've heard him!"

"You must be Leggy." the Visitor wondered if it was in order for him to use what was so obviously a nickname, but he had no other at his disposal. "I am......."

"Don't worry, I know who you bastard well are," Leggy interrupted him again, "I'll just get this little bastard sorted out for you."

With his vision now fully adapted to the poor light the Visitor was able to see what was being sorted out. Leggy was pouring cider from a barrel into a three handled china cup, the size of which the Visitor had never seen before in his life. He guessed that it must hold about half a gallon and in this he guessed correctly, the vessel being known in this part of the country as a 'God–forgive-me'. Realising that mine host in Paradise was not intending to beat him up, the Visitor would have liked to strike up a conversation with the man. Having been interrupted twice already, however, he had a suspicion that such an attempt at discourse would fail. Instead he waited in silence until the over–sized cider pot was filled and then lifted up onto the counter.

"Fiver," said Leggy, holding his hand out for the money, "and if that little bastard gets broken you can pay for it!"

After handing over the required payment and lifting the God–forgive-me from the bar the Visitor found himself walking more cautiously away from Paradise than he had towards it. For not only was the giant cider cup heavy and filled to the brim, he also had Leggy's warning about breakages ringing in his ears. Had he but known, this threat was not as dire as it seemed: the vessel, if it got broken, could be replaced fairly cheaply. A 'God–forgive-me' was not generally available commercially, usually such items could only be found in an antique shop. Once popular amongst farm labourers, who would gather in a barn during the evenings to share gossip and cider, their use belonged to a bygone age. Their introduction to Paradise was the purely accidental innovation of the master craftsman at a nearby pottery. Being rather fond of a drink himself he had once created a 'God–forgive-me' and had, for amusement, taken it into Paradise and requested that it be filled. Leggy's first reaction was one of amazement at the size of the vessel and this was the only effect intended by its maker. Once word of this usefully sized cider cup spread amongst the regulars in Paradise however, the potter received many requests for more to be produced. This he was quite happy to do at little cost, quite often no more than in exchange for a few drinks, until eventually Leggy adopted them as standard use for his hostelry. At this juncture a deal was struck whereby Paradise would be kept supplied with these pots in exchange for a comparative amount of drinks on the house. Such was the track record for breakages here that at times the potter was kept very busy with this private work but, fortunately, he considered it a labour of love. The craft of the potter was his pleasure as well as his work, to combine his skill with the occasional free pot of cider he viewed as a bonus.

The regular cider drinkers themselves were impressed with this decision. To those who knew how to fully appreciate this beverage there was no other way of drinking it apart from a china cup. To this end they each had been in the habit of keeping their own personal pots behind the bar: a pint pot for a quick drink and a quart pot for more a extended session. Now they also had the choice of a house 'God–forgive-me' for when they wished to indulge in the laziness of less trips to the bar for refills. The vessel was made with three handles, equally spaced, for the simple reason that it was originally intended to be a shared cup. This design was ideal for passing the 'God–forgive-me' around a circle of drinkers. But the greatest delight to the users of these giant pots in Paradise was due to their source. As the master craftsman worked at a pottery whose reputation reached worldwide for their quality products, the cider drinkers in Paradise could hold their cups up high and state, proudly;

"The posh folks might look at us as if we're covered in shit, but we only drinks from the finest pots!"

And so it was that a fine pot was duly presented to Boathook Bald, filled with the day's liquid reward which would loosen his tongue. Once the 'God–forgive-me' had been carefully set down upon the bench between them the Visitor witnessed the sight of cider appreciation in its purest form. The prawnman leaned his head towards the vessel until his lips met the rim. He then swallowed several large gulps without the need to raise the cup: a testament to the Visitor's success in transporting the golden nectar without spilling a drop. Golden nectar that the seasoned cider drinkers in Paradise referred to as 'Milk of Amnesia'.

As Boathook Bald then raised his head he closed his eyes, smiling and licking his lips noisily. The taste of fermented apples was transporting him to late summertime orchards and delight showed clear in his expression. For an instant the Visitor felt envy: he too would go where the prawnman found such sheer pleasure, it was if this nirvana was so close that he could reach out and touch it. Unfortunately this instant was rudely broken by a voice nearby;

"Why, good morrow to you my brave Captain."

The Visitor felt his heart sink and his hair rise at his sudden ejection from nirvana. So intent had he been on his fetching and carrying that he had failed to notice Lucy

Love stood watching him from a short distance away. Nor had he been aware of her approach to the spot where he was now sitting. As he turned to face her it was not with bravery nor anything like it, as the beads of sweat which broke out across his brow indicated. She was dressed in much the same way as she had been on the previous day although, in place of the paraffin, she now carried a hurricane lamp. This she now held up for his inspection, the centre of her lips moving slightly as she did so;

"Look." She commanded, inclining her head towards the lamp.

"It's, er, very nice." Her brave Captain replied whilst at the same time wishing that the ground would open and swallow her up.

"It's for you."

She would have smiled as she said this, but doing so would have ruined a complexion which appeared to have been the work of a skilled plasterer. Instead she widened her eyes very slightly, a signal to her beau that his enthusiastic response was awaited. She was taken much by surprise therefore when his mouth fell open and issued forth a confused babble;

"It's very kind of you but really shouldn't have done... no, really....I could not accept such a magnificent gift...no, really...er, much as I appreciate it of course..but, no, really.... you shouldn't have."

He stopped speaking, suddenly aware that something was amiss. Although the strange woman had said that the lamp was for him, she showed no sign of actually handing it over: she was just holding it up for him to look at. All that he could now do, under the beam of the love-light in her eyes, was resort to a sickly grin and wait to see what happened next.

"It's not a gift, Silly Billy!" Lucy squealed in delight, viewing his misunderstanding as an endearing trait which made her love him all the more. With these words she carefully blew him a kiss and then turned and went on her way.

She left Silly Billy more confused than he had been on the previous day. As he watched her walking away towards the quay, still holding the hurricane lamp gaily aloft, his mind was trying and failing to decide whether or not he was losing his sanity. In this inner turmoil he quite forgot that he had company: so much so that when the voice of the prawnman broke into his train of thought the startled Visitor let forth an involuntary yelp.

"What 'ave y'been up to?" Boathook Bald demanded to know, "Y'been an' got y'self tied up with our Lucy?"

"No, not at all!" The Visitor turned to face his accuser, his confused brain clutching at the strand of hope that had just been offered to him, though the last had clearly been voiced as a statement rather than a question.

"I mean, after all, she is your Lucy and you must keep her. Anyway, enough about me. How did you get on with your fishing yesterday?"

"Never mind 'bout that," the reply was spoken firmly, "'ow come y'got y'self engaged to Lucy Love?"

"Oh, is that her name? Well, I don't know.... that is to say, I'm not. I'm not engaged to her."

"Jus' 'ang on a minute." Boathook Bald leant forward to have another long swallow of his cider. Then, refreshed, he carried on with his line of enquiry. "If y'aint told 'er that y'goin' t'marry 'er she wouldn't 'ave got you a lamp. An' if she didn't think y'was a ships' Cap'n she wouldn't want t'marry you. What 'ave y'been up to?"

With the prawnman's reference to a ship's Captain the

unwilling Romeo suddenly understood much. It was the wearing of his father's uniform which had caused a betrothal to be thrust upon him: now he knew how but not why. He realised that he was going to have to give an explanation about the circumstances under which he met Lucy Love the previous day. One detail which, for sheer embarrassment, he would leave out would be his mode of dress. But before he explained anything he felt quite justified in asking exactly who Lucy Love was and what was the significance of the lantern.

"Ah, Lucy Love." The prawnman seemed quite happy to provide an explanation. "If I told y'ev'rythin' I knew 'bout 'er then y'd know a thing or two, an' I'm tellin' y'that f'r nothin'! Story is that when she were just a lass, 'bout seventeen, she was walkin' 'long the quay one day an' she met a ship's Cap'n. 'is ship 'ad jus' come 'longside y'see. Well, they looked at each other an' fell straightaway in love, like folks do in books only this was f'r real. They do say y'never saw a pair so in love with each other, they was out walkin' 'and in 'and all over the place. O'course there then come the day when 'is ship 'ad to sail an' they was both 'eartbroken. Now then, they reckon that with their last goodbyes they made promises t'each other. 'e swore that one day 'e would come back an' marry 'er. An' then she told 'im that ev'ry ev'nin', when it got dark, she would go down t'the Fisherman's Dock an' light a lantern for 'im."

Here the prawnman paused, realising that the significance of this would need elaborating upon. Further elaboration was something that required another gulp of cider of course, so the pause was extended to include this necessity.

"When a ship comes in at night a reg'lar Cap'n knows all o'the lights on the shore an' if anythin' 'as changed 'e'll know it straightaway. An' that's because the shore lights 'elp 'im nav'gate through the 'arbour y'see. So Lucy knew that 'er lantern would be seen by 'im a'soon as 'is ship come in at night y'see. She told 'im that this would be a signal to 'im that 'er love was still burnin' bright."

"What a lovely story." remarked the Visitor, although he was quite unable to equate the apparition that he had recently encountered as a sweet lass of seventeen.

"An' that lantern was useful f'r the fishermen too," the prawnman continued, "if they was out there in the dark an' it was time t'head back they would use that light y'see, they jus' 'ad t'look for it an' it would lead them straight back into Fisherman's Dock. It became known as 'Lucy's Lantern'. Anyway, back t'the story, Lucy was b'side 'erself with grief at 'is goin'. 'specially when she realised that when 'e said 'bout comin' back one day 'e 'adn't actu'lly said which day that was goin' t'be. So after waitin' f'r a week she give up on 'im. Then she got 'erself all dressed up in 'er best an' went off down the quay t'fall in love with 'nother Cap'n. She got a dredger Skipper that time, 'is ship was in f'r repairs so that was lucky. They got 'bout three weeks of the bein' in love afore 'e 'ad t'sail away y'see. An' it were the self same story all over again, 'e says the comin' back t'marry 'er bit an' she says 'bout the lantern. So then she is down at Fisherman's Dock ev'ry ev'nin' lightin' up two lanterns, one f'r each of 'em y'see."

"Well then, over the years she's fell in love with the Cap'ns of all sorts o'ships. Tankers, coal boats, sand ships, Customs cutters, Royal Navy, you name it she fell in love with 'em! Y'see, she's never twigged that they aint ever comin' back an' they all got their own lantern. O'course the upshot o'this is that she's down at the Dock ev'ry night with eighty-odd lanterns. It takes 'er the best part of an 'our to get 'em all lit up an' a right 'azard to navigatin' they are too! 'Lucy's

Bloody Lights' we calls 'em."

The prawnman paused and threw the Visitor a sharp accusing look.

"But she's only ever fell in love with ship's Cap'ns. We 'as a sayin' down 'ere; 'If y'sits on the quay 'oldin' a bit o'bread then a seagull's goin' t'shit on you.' Meanin' y'must've done somethin' t'draw 'er attention on y'self!"

The Visitor knew that he was going to have to give an account of his first meeting with Lucy Love. This he did, omitting to mention that he had been wearing his father's naval uniform at the time. Instead he feigned bafflement as to the reason why he should be mistaken for a ship's Captain. At the end of this explanation of the events of the previous day he expressed concern about the woman's belief in their engagement. His confidante was fully aware that he had not been told, nor was he likely to be told, the full story. Yet he was willing to let the matter go with a great roar of laughter;

"Don't y'go worryin' 'bout that! We reckons that by now if one of 'er Cap'ns did try an' marry 'er she'd run a mile. I don't s'pose you'll see 'er again now she got you engaged, an' if y'do jus' smile an' nod an' agree with anythin' she says. She aint goin' t'take it no further, 'er life is too devoted t'lookin' after all 'em bloody lanterns t'be 'avin' an 'usband on board!"

He laughed again, looking at the Visitor and shaking his head.

"Fancy you askin' 'er if she knew the Vicar! Say things like that t'Lucy Love an' she thinks y'talkin' weddin's. Anyway, seein' as 'ow we're talkin' 'bout weddin's, I'll tell you 'bout some o'the traditions when we 'as a prawnin' fam'ly one. We don't go 'bout it like other folks do y'see."

The Visitor felt both relief and gratitude in equally

high measures at the turn-around in his status with regard to Lucy Love. In order to fully savour the pleasure of his newfound freedom he waited patiently whilst Boathook Bald took some refreshment from the 'God–forgive-me'. After much noisy slurping, swallowing, wiping of drips from his whiskers and a tiny belch, the prawnman was finally capable of speech. He began with a somewhat surprising statement;

"When my gran'father died recently he'd not long 'ad 'is 'undredth weddin' an'versary. 'ow 'bout that?"

"Well, that really is something." The receiver of this news felt his eyebrows rising, "So how old was your grandfather when he passed away?"

"'e was an 'undred years old! Y'see, it's on account o'one o'our traditions. When one o'us gets born the day of our weddin', an' who we're goin' t'marry, is decided straight'way by our gran'mother. It's 'er job to work this out an' write it in the big fam'ly book."

"The big family book?" queried the Visitor.

"That's right. Y'see, down 'ere we don't like strangers, beggin' y'pardon sir. So in the prawnin' fam'lies we don't get ourselves married t'nobody who aint in 'nother prawnin' fam'ly. It keeps it so we're all r'lated t'each other some'ow. O'course, y'aint allowed t'go gettin' wed t'nobody who's too closely r'lated 'cos then there's problems. So t'stop this 'appenin' each fam'ly 'as a book, 'The Big Fam'ly Book' it's called, an' it shows who's related t'who an' 'ow. Now then, when one o'us gets born its gran'mother looks in the book t'see who it c'n get married t'when it grows up. Then that gets written in the book y'see an' the ol' lady will also pick the date o'the weddin'. An' t'make it more special we don't get told who we goin' to wed with. That's like a surprise on the day y'see. But we all knows our weddin' day right from bein' tiny an' so we c'n 'ave our an'versary ev'ry year. Most of us're up t'our Silver by the time we actu'lly gets wed."

"So it's like an arranged marriage?" The Visitor was incredulous. "I would never have thought such a thing! What happens if you do not like the partner chosen for you?"

Now it was the prawnman's turn to look incredulous, such a notion had never occurred to him and to hear it spoken caused him great bafflement;

"O'course you're goin' t'be 'appy with y'gran'mothers' choice!" he spoke these words as one stating a fundamental truth which was beyond question. "It would be mos' disr'spec'ful otherwise, an' we all gets taught 'bout r'spectin' our fam'ly an' our traditions. Now then, I know I got t'be p'lite t'you but I won't listen to nothin' that's got disr'spec' in it. I know our way of doin' things may not be ev'ry ones cup'o'tea but it's 'ow we likes t'do it! An' apart from anythin' else, if we was left t'go an' find our own partner it wouldn' 'appen'. We're too busy at the prawnin' y'see, an' that's what the city folks don't understand. Our traditions are there 'cos we needs 'em an' they're there t'make sure we gets looked after!"

The Visitor felt no little shame at the lack of tact which had caused the prawnman to become so defensive: it certainly had not been the intention. Inwardly he admonished himself for such carelessness, it showed a lack of sensitivity unforgivable in one who needed to maintain a good rapport with his informants. Rather than to attempt an apology, which he knew full well could only serve to make the situation worse, he sought for a way to steer Boathook Bald into calmer waters. He glanced down and, to his relief, noted that the prawnman was wearing a wedding ring. This thin band of gold gave the Visitor the excuse he needed whilst still keeping the subject of the weddings active:

"I fully agree that people should keep these traditions alive," was the only comment he allowed himself for the pacification of the prawnman, "so tell me about your wedding day. It will be an ideal way for me to get a better picture of these traditions."

"Ah, now then, my weddin' day was a strange one, meanin' it wasn't like the usual ones y'see. When I was born my gran'mother looked into the book an' couldn't find anyone f'r me t'marry. They do say that f'r a while back then too many boys got 'emselves born. This was a big problem an' no two ways 'bout it! First off 'cos I got t'ave a weddin' an'versary like ev'ryone else but also 'cos she got t'make sure I marries into the fam'ly y'see. So after thinkin' 'bout it for a bit gran'mother come up with the perfec' s'lution, I would 'ave t'marry m'self."

"To yourself?" Suddenly the Visitor was struggling not to repeat his earlier lack of diplomacy. Subduing any thoughts of doubting the truth of the prawnman's words, he instead phrased his next question carefully; "I should have thought that perhaps the Vicar conducting the service...."

"Oh, we don't do none o'that vicarin' stuff." interrupted the prawnman, "When we gets married we does it on the boat an' the Master does the marryin' f'r us. That's our tradition y'see. So I turns up on the day 'spectin' t'see a bride only there wasn't one an' that's when I foun' out what gran'mother 'ad done. Master Miles says t'me, 'Don't worry Bald, I'll change a few words an' you c'n go away married', an' that's what 'e very kin'ly did an' I got wed t'm'self. O'course, it's very 'spensive gettin' y'self married, Master says that's so you takes it serious an' looks proper t'y'responsibil'ties y'see. It meant I 'ad t'work mos' o'that season f'r nothin' so I could pay Master f'r the cer'mony. But t'was worth it f'r such a lov'ly day."

Boathook Bald paused to smile at what were obviously very happy memories. Then, as if in confirmation of this, he lifted up the huge cup as if proposing a toast;

"Here's t'bein' wed, a fine thing!" He announced before putting the 'God–forgive-me' to his lips to take a huge gulp of the cider.

The Visitor, although still incredulous, could see that he was being told the truth about the prawnman's wedding. He looked down at his notepad: more so than before he wondered what on earth they would make of all of this back at the office. This train of thought was finally halted by the prawnman ceasing his gazing at far off days and resuming his talking about them;

"Trouble was, Durin' the cer'mony I used all my word 'lowance so I couldn't get t'thank the Master aft'wards."

"Word allowance? Sorry to interrupt, what is a word allowance?" asked the Visitor.

"Well, this is one o'our traditions y'see. When y'sign on for a season with a Master 'e gives a word 'lowance. That's 'ow many words y'c'n speak ev'ry week on the boat. Master Miles says that if the crewman was talkin' too much it gives the Master a bad 'ead 'avin' to 'ear it y'see. So part of the 'greement f'r the job is y'r word 'lowance, I gets twenty-five a week which is very gen'rous, but that's on account o' Master Miles bein' kind t'me, some o'the lads only gets two or three y'know. An' once you used up all y'words then y'aint t'speak t'the Master no more that week. Now then, Master Miles worked out the cer'mony so that ev'rythin' I 'ad t'say could be done within a weeks' 'lowance. You show me a Vicar that'd do that f'r you! You can't 'cos there aint one, that's why we don't go for none of that vicarin' y'see. But that Master Miles made it a lov'ly cer'mony an' I did enjoy bein' married. I got proper upset when I foun' out I 'ad t'get a divorce."

"You...er, sorry....divorce?"

"Yes." The prawnman looked sad, "It's me own fault an' I can't blame nobody else. I aint proud o'what I did, I was unfaithful. There, now I've told you an' if that makes y'think any less o'me then it's no more'n what I d'serves!"

The Visitor, in truth, did not know what to think. Within, he was feeling two very strong urges: the first was demanding that he should immediately go to a secluded place and scream, it was telling him that this was all that was required to make the world seem sane once more.

But he also had his professional calling to counteract this extreme measure. While still trying to fully come to terms with the fact that this man had married himself, it had suddenly been thrust upon him that his divorce had occurred too. He had a job to do, for this reason alone he knew that he would have to coax further explanation from this wayward husband;

"No, I do not think any less of you, we all make mistakes. Perhaps it would be good for you to talk about it?

"Well, t'was at the 'Breakwater Leap' las' year." Boathook Bald glanced at his new-found counsellor, "y'don't know what that is, do you? That's 'cos it's one o'our traditions that don't 'appen anywhere else in the world 'cept 'ere. Now then, if y'goes down t'the Fishermans' Dock y'will see that it's pr'tected by a breakwater. At the quay end of it there's plenty o'water, so then the bigger boats c'n get in an' out whatever the tide's doin'. But down the other end there aint much water at all, 'specially when the tide goes out. An' when we gets the lowest o'the springs it's only 'bout five foot across from the shore t'the breakwater. Now then, once a year all the crewmen from the Prawnin' Fleet gets down there f'r the 'Breakwater Leap', this is like a comp'tition y'see. You gets a good low water an' we sees who c'n jump over t'the breakwater an' back mos' times without gettin' their waders wet. Gettin' over is easy 'cos you c'n take a run at it down the shore y'see. But then gettin' back y' 'as t'use y'boat'ook t'vault across. Get y'waders wet more'n three times an' you're out an' that's the skill of it, keepin' 'em dry. It gets 'arder as the tide comes back in 'cos then the gap gets wider y'see.

We makes a proper day of it, The 'Breakwater Leap' is a day f'r us t''be larkin' 'bout an' we don't get many o'them. Lots o'the townsfolk comes t'watch us an' the Masters bring their fam'lies 'long too. The kids love it, y'should see their little faces light up when one o'us slips on the seaweed an' breaks an ankle. An' o'course the Masters likes t''ave a wager or two on it. Like I said, a proper day of it! An' it aint over when the tide comes in an' we got t'put an end t'the leapin', then we 'as music 'an dancin' up on the 'ard t'see the day out. We gets a fire goin' an' Leggy sends us down some cider so we c'n 'ave a few drinks. An' that's where I got t'know Meg."

The prawnman paused in order to lift the 'God–forgive-me' to his lips. After a generous swallow from its contents, he wiped the residue cider from his beard and then continued.

"None o'the lads liked t'ask 'er t'dance 'cos they all reckon she's got a face like a sackful o'whelks, but I foun' 'er sweet 'nough. T'was all innocent t'start with, I jus' thought it'd be like 'avin' a jig or two an' that's all there was to it - none o'that funny business. An' we did 'ave a lot o'fun t'gether at the dancin'. But I sup'ose with a couple of drinks inside o'me I sort o'f'rgot meself an' at the end I give 'er a kiss. I don't 'spect it were a proper kiss 'cos I 'adn't done it afore an' I wern't sure 'ow t'do it right. But that was me undoin' y'see 'cos word got out 'bout it. When Master Miles 'eard what I'd done I thought 'e was goin' t'keel'aul me! 'e said I'd made a mockery o'marr'age an' I'd well an' truly broke me vows. Then I think 'e must've took pity on me 'cos 'e said that, as 'e'd been the one t'sort out the weddin', 'e'd sort out me divorce. I was grateful t"im f'r that 'cos I wouldn't know 'ow t'go 'an get one. O'course I 'ad t'work a whole season for 'im with no pay 'cos of 'is costs in the matter. But like 'e says t'me at the time, the whole thing could've got a lot nastier if I'd 'ad t'go an' see the legal people an' tell them what I'd done!"

Boathook Bald paused again and stared reflectively at a dead seagull laying in a nearby gutter. The Visitor let him sit in silence, realising that these memories were very painful for the poor man. If it were not for the fact that he found the overall concept of marriage and divorce in the prawning families so surreal he may have felt pity. As it was he just experienced the first stirrings of another of his headaches.

"Anyways," The prawnman snapped suddenly out of his musings with a smile upon his face, "it all turned out a'right in the end. Y'see, gran'mother must've been a bit un'appy 'bout 'avin' nobody f'r me t'marry. When I got born there was a couple of lasses that would've done f'r me but they was already spoke for. The ol' lady did put a note in the book t'say that if anythin' 'appened to any o'the lads lined up for 'em then I was t'step in 'an take 'is place. So when Marty Green disappeared that left a lass that I c'n marry one day. Master Miles says I got t'let all the fuss 'bout me divorce settle down first though, says t'wouldn't be right t'rush it."

"What happened to Marty Green?" the Visitor wanted to know, "How did he come to disappear?"

"The daft sod got 'imself pissed up one day an' took it into 'is 'ead t'go an' 'unt the Great White Prawn." answered Boathook Bald. "An' that's the las' we seen of 'im!"

"What is......? The Visitor started to ask.

"The Great White Prawn?" The prawnman finished the sentence for him." Well, there's some as says 'e don't exist an' some as says 'e do exist. But if y'ask a prawnman, 'e'll tell y"e do exist. I knows 'e does 'cos I seen 'im. Not all of 'im mind, 'cos 'e don't show 'imself prop'ly t'folks, but ev'ry so often, out there on the Prawnin' Groun's, y'catch a glimpse o'somethin' out o'the corner of y'eye an' y'jus' knows it's 'im. 'e's a cock prawn an' 'e's 'bout six foot long."

Boathook Bald looked at the Visitor full in the eyes with an expression that defied any contradiction of the existence of this great beast. If the prawnman's audience of one felt any amusement he kept it well hidden: this latest divulgence promised to be an interesting addition to the day's business. There was, however, a question that he needed to ask;

"What is a cock prawn?"

"Don't y'know?" The question took Boathook Bald by surprise, it being his belief that certain things were common knowledge, "Prawns, well, all shellfish, is 'ens or cocks. Meanin' female or male y'see."

"I beg your pardon." the Visitor responded, "No, I didn't know that. You learn something new every day, as they say. But, please, carry on with your story. I find it quite fascinating."

Of course, carrying on with the story could only be accomplished after an attack upon the cider. This act the prawnman carried out with great relish. Once his thirst had been quenched, Boathook Bald set the 'God-forgive-me' back onto the bench and proceeded to further enlighten the Visitor.

"Well, they do say that years and years ago the Great White Prawn was jus' like any other prawn. Then one day 'e did King Neptune a great favour. Ol' Neptune was so grateful f'r this that in return 'e b'stowed 'pon the little feller some special powers. That were it! The prawn could live forever an' 'e grew an' 'e grew 'til 'e was as big as Neptune 'imself! An' as 'e grew 'e changed colour 'til 'e was pure white. Then Neptune says 'e could be in charge o'that part o'the sea y'see. It was 'is job t'keeps an eye on all o'the Kings subjects there an' make sure that everythin' was a'right. Neptune also told 'im that 'is special powers would protect 'im, that no other creature would be able t'go 'unt 'im. That's why, when we are out in the boat, we never says 'Great White Prawn' out loud cos if 'e 'ears us say that 'e might think we're 'untin' 'im. If we do 'ave t'say anythin' 'bout 'im we got a nickname that we uses - we calls 'im 'Moby Cock.'"

"But Marty Green did go and hunt him." noted the Visitor.

"Ah, well, 'e tried, but 'e didn't get very far! Y'see, that day Marty 'ad been on a good session, skullin' cider since breakfas' time. Now when Marty did that 'e would end up gettin' all big 'eaded, start tellin' ev'ryone 'ow great 'e was an' reckonin' that 'e could do anythin'. That were jus' 'is way y'see an' none 'eld it against 'im. B'sides, after a bit o'this 'e'd gen'rally jus' fall asleep an' then we knew we'd get some peace. But on that p'tic'lar day 'e started goin' on 'bout 'ow 'e was goin' t'go out an' catch the Great White Prawn. O'course ev'ryone was jus' 'avin' a laugh at 'im, or at least they was 'til 'e sud'nly upped an' marched off down t'the dock. When they re'lised 'e was actu'lly goin' out in 'is boat they tries t'stop 'im. They was wantin' t'talk 'im out o' it y'see. O'course, Marty bein' Marty, 'e were 'avin' none o'that an' off 'e went. They do say it were a beaut'ful day, flat calm an' as clear as y'like. But they reckon all that changed a'soon as 'e got near t'the prawnin' groun's. Sud'nly a thick fog comes down all aroun' 'im, an' it were so bad 'e couldn't even see as far as the end o''is nose! Now then, this should've been a warnin' to 'im t'leave well alone, but that wasn't 'is way. Once 'e got started on these daft ideas 'e felt obliged to see 'em through or 'e'd lose face y'see. So 'e carried on, gettin' all 'is gear ready so that once the fog lifted 'e could set 'bout 'is 'unting. Trouble was, the fog didn't lift. Instead it got all blown away by a 'uge gale that sprung up from nowhere! Now then, y'got t'bear in mind that weather conditions like this is un'eard of' an' there aint nothin' in nature that c'n cause 'em. If that wasn't Ol' Neptune protectin' the Great White Prawn then let y'tell me what it was. But y'can't an' that's all there is to it!"

Despite having the sea in his blood (although the many years that he had spent in an office meant that this had been somewhat diluted by correction fluid) the Visitor could not provide an alternative explanation. Nor did he wish to try: his initial scepticism as to the existence of the creature had been replaced by a total absorption in what he was being told, the prawnmans' sincerity was giving the tale no little credibility. By now totally caught up in relating the story, Boathook Bald started waving his arms about as he described the effects of the gale.

"They do say that Marty Green could do nothin' 'cept hold on f'dear life, 'is boat was gettin' thrown 'bout all over the place! Waves as big as 'ouses was crashin' down on 'im! It was terrifyin' an' 'e was terrified out o' 'is wits by it. They do reckon that by the end o'the storm Marty 'ad come t'look like the Great White Prawn 'imself. 'is 'air 'ad turned white, 'is skin 'ad turned white an' they d'say it were so bad that even 'is teeth 'ad turned white! An' the boat was gettin' so filled up with water that 'e knew it mus' sink, so 'e grabs a life-ring an' jumps overboard."

"And then he disappeared?" asked the awestruck Visitor,

so wrapped up in this story that he was almost forgetting to breathe. "They never found him?"

"Ah, well now, 'ere's a strange thing." The prawnman adopted the expression of one who had pondered upon a mystery for many hours without ever finding a satisfactory explanation. "The boat didn't sink. 'stead it got took by the wind an' tide over t'the west 'til it got washed ashore, an' by rights Marty should've been taken the same way. But 'e didn't! 'e got carried off t'the east an' that don't make no sense neither. 'e was blown by some unnat'ral force into the wrong d'rection y'see. Away t'the east 'e went, swearin' that never again would 'e drink the cider if only Ol' Neptune let 'im live. Eventu'lly o'course the sea calmed down an' 'e was able t'swim ashore. Then 'e disappeared. 'e aint never goin' t'be seen 'ere no more an' they reckon that somethin' 'orrible 'appened to Marty Green."

Here Boathook Bald's eyes widened in disbelief at the thought of this new terror which had befallen the foolishly headstrong prawnman: his voice dropped to a near whisper, as if speaking of such ill fortune could bring bad luck down upon his own head;

"They d'say that Marty Green ended up livin' in Bournemouth!"

Chapter Eight

Master Miles sat at the main table in The Club ignoring a cup of coffee which was going cold. One of his responsibilities as Admiral of the Fleet was to deal with any mail addressed to the Prawning Masters as a body and this he was now doing. One particular item of correspondence needed rather more of his attention than the others, he found himself having to read and re-read it several times in order to fully comprehend its implications. Increasingly this was causing him to click his tongue and to shake his head from side to side slowly. Also in The Club that morning were three other Masters of the Prawning Fleet and each were aware that something was not to their Admiral's liking. He was, however, so obviously deep in thought that in deference to his position they kept their silence. He would speak to them when he was ready to do so. In the meantime they exchanged worried glances with each other: so unusual was it for Master Miles to be thus concerned about anything so trivial as the contents of a letter.

Finally, with the expulsion of breath blown heavily from within puffed cheeks, the letter was dropped upon the table. The Admiral glanced at his colleagues briefly before standing up and walking across to the windows. Here he stood with his back to them for a few minutes as he appeared to be casually observing the activity outside. But this picture of one relaxed as he took in the sights of a busy quayside was betrayed by the subtle agitated movements of his body: the rocking backwards and forwards on the soles of his feet, the hands clasped tightly behind his back to stop them from fidgeting, these were the outward signs that something was seriously amiss. Finally, and so suddenly that it made the other Masters start, he turned and made the reason for his disquiet known.

"Gentlemen, we have a problem. A big problem. The lease on this place is up for renewal." Here he paused and waved a hand to indicate the premises in which they were all stood. "This has not had to be done for a long time, certainly not in my time with the Fleet. I was aware that this was coming up and I did not envisage any reason why this should not happen as a matter of course. However, something that I was not aware of is that the land upon which this building stands was once the property of the Church. This was many centuries ago, as we will all know from our local history lessons at school. But it seems that when the Church authorities released the land they put certain covenants upon the deeds of sale. These stated what could or could not go on within any buildings which were subsequently erected here. Are you all with me so far?"

His three avid listeners nodded and one of them observed; "Where is the problem though? The Prawning Masters have held the lease for generation upon generation. There has not, to my knowledge at least, ever been any question regarding what we use it for. And it is not exactly something that we shout from the masthead!"

"The problem is," Master Miles walked back over to the table speaking slowly and with great emphasis, "that in order to ensure that the Churches' wishes are met, each time the lease is renewed it has to be ratified by the local Vicar. In this instance The Reverend Michael Grape."

The effect of this revelation upon his small audience was

one of immediate concern: the ramifications did not need to be spelt out to them. They were each moved to give a verbal response;

"Good grief!"
"Good heavens!"
"Oh shit!"

None of which quite conveyed the enormity of the dilemma that they now faced. Master Miles walked back over to the window and once again stared out at the quay. Without turning to face them, he resumed speaking to his fellow Masters.

"I hardly need to remind you that it is not the custom of the Prawning Fleet to be told by anybody what we can and cannot do. Certainly not through words on an antiquated scrap of paper which should be consigned to the museum vaults where it belongs!"

With these words he spun around and flicked a contemptuous finger at the offending letter, sending it fluttering across the table and onto the floor.

"Gentlemen, this is a serious situation: I want every Master in the Fleet to meet here this evening at twenty hundred hours, let it be known that my instructions are for no absentees. There is no time to lose in sifting through this messy business before that madman in the Vicarage gets his teeth into it. In the meantime I have to go and catch the tide, I have some of last years pots to retrieve. No doubt you all do too, but I make it your priority to pass the word around the Masters. I will have every one of them sat at this table tonight, or if not I will know the reason why!"

The Admiral walked out of the room with only the briefest of farewells to his colleagues. He knew that when he returned at the appointed time that evening all of the Masters would be there. He also knew that they would be looking to him to provide a solution to the crisis that they faced: at the moment he did not have one. As he stepped out of the building and into the glare of the sun reflecting off of the water between the quays, he cursed inwardly at the unfortunate timing of the news he had just received: Chick Bateman had departed these shores and returned to his home in France. Now, more than ever before, would he have appreciated the older man's counsel.

Walking along the Town Quay towards the Fisherman's Dock Master Miles recalled his limited dealings with The Reverend Michael Grape. Quite why this fiery preacher disliked the Prawnmen so vehemently was a mystery to them. Furthermore, until this day none of them had cared to know: they had viewed the Vicar as a harmless eccentric, a figure of fun whose presence in the town impinged upon their lives not one iota. Now, it appeared, he could step in and close The Club, the collective symbol of the high standing which they enjoyed in the town. To Master Miles himself the situation also carried a more personal threat, that of damage to his reputation. If the Prawning Fleet lost their pride whilst he was their Admiral he would be burdened with shame for the rest of his days. He had to come up with an answer, a solution that would not only save their honour but would enhance his own. For the moment, however, his total lack of any such remedy was putting him into a very fragile humour.

But upon reaching the Fisherman's Dock he had to put aside such worries: there was a job to be done, namely the recovery of his lost prawn pots. Such losses occurred when the length of rope that attached a pot to a cork float became caught around a rock below the surface of the sea. Usually when this happened it was possible for the crewman to lean over the side of the boat and, by deft use of his boathook, free the rope. In practised hands this operation could be successfully completed within seconds. But this simple task was not always so effective in recovering a pot and every season saw two or three pots stuck fast. In order to save the expense of replacing this most basic piece of equipment it was necessary to wait for an exceptionally low tide. With luck rocks that spent most of the year under the water would then be exposed to the air and the crewman could clamber among them freeing the ensnared pots by hand. As a suitable tide was predicted for that day Master Miles had sent a message to Boathook Bald telling him to meet him at the dock, along with this message had been another apologising to the Visitor for any inconvenience that this may cause. As the crewman had arrived shortly before his Master, the prawning vessel was being made ready to leave its mooring. This efficiency in preparing for their work did nothing to help the Admiral's frame of mind; indeed, he stepped aboard as if not even aware of what he was doing, so preoccupied was he. As the *'Prudence'* got under way and carried the two prawnmen out of the harbour toward the prawning grounds, Boathook Bald sensed his Master's gloom. Made foolish by the amount of cider that he had consumed that morning, he had attempted various acts of cheerfulness to alleviate this melancholy, acts which were made more ridiculous by their having to be performed silently in order to comply with the crewman's weekly word allowance. Thus, hornpipes were danced accompanied by the pulling of facial expressions which, in other circumstances, may have caused mild amusement at the very least. These efforts were, however, abruptly curtailed by the Admiral with the threat of an anchor being inserted anally into the crewman. As this dire threat carried much force in its voicing the rest of the voyage to the prawning grounds passed in a nervous silence.

Arriving at their destination they found themselves in the company of other prawning vessels engaged in the same activity. The successful recovery of these pots at the start of the season meant that the Masters would have time to take stock of their gear and replace any that were lost completely. Master Miles and Boathook Bald set to their work with haste, needing to complete the task before the tide turned and submerged the rocks once more. Whilst the Fleet's crewmen toiled, crawling amongst the slippery seaweed covered rocks, the Masters cast surreptitious glances into each other's boats. They were most concerned to ensure that none of their colleagues retrieved any pots that were not their own whilst, at the same time, hoping to get away with playing this same trick themselves.

~~*~~

The Reverend Michael Grape sat at the desk in his study opening a pile of mail delivered that morning. This consisted entirely of correspondence on matters of Church business: he dealt with his own private letters at the breakfast table, thus ensuring that once he started his day's duties nothing would interfere with God's work. The opening of each envelope revealed the mundane paperwork involved with the running of his Parish or the upkeep of the Church itself. Except one: this, the last that he had opened, contained three sheets of foolscap paper. Two of these were filled with line after line of legal jargon, which he could not straightaway understand, whilst the third had a small section of a street-map printed on it. A cursory glance at the names of the streets told him that the map was of part of the town, though he was not entirely sure exactly where they were located. He also noted that certain buildings were shown, one of which had been highlighted in red ink.

Calling out to Mrs Fountain, his housekeeper, to bring him a cup of coffee he took these papers over to his armchair. Here, in front of a warming log fire, he could sit comfortably while he tried to make some sense of them. Despite being a well educated man he, like most people, found legal documents intimidating. He shared the commonly held view that the complicated wording and phrasing they contained was for one purpose only: to pull the wool over the eyes of the uninitiated. But he knew that the documents in his hand related to Church business, therefore it was his duty to read them and to comprehend their secrets. By painfully slow study he had managed to understand them in part in the time that it took for his coffee to arrive. They told him that, for some as yet inexplicable reason, his signature was required on some leases that were due for renewal. His curiosity was now making him wonder where and why. To the first of these questions the answer was close at hand;

"Mrs Fountain," he said, holding up the street-map for the housekeeper to see, "You are from this town, I wonder if you could tell me what these buildings are, the ones highlighted in red?"

The housekeeper, pleased to be asked to share what little knowledge she possessed, took the paper and studied it closely for a few seconds before announcing;

"I'll have to put me reading glasses on!"

Reaching into her apron pocket she extracted a pair of spectacles which she then held up in front of her eyes without putting them on properly. The Vicar observed that only the right eye had a lens in it, the left lens was missing, and seeing the Vicar notice this caused Mrs Fountain to feel that an explanation was needed;

"I didn't like the left one so I took it out and threw it away,

I just couldn't get on with it at all. I never liked that optician much anyway. His wife makes cakes for the Church fete and she never puts the right amount of sugar in, always to much or not enough that's her. Mind you he's plagued with boils, only ever has one at a time but, goodness me, the size of them! And he..."

"The map Mrs Fountain?" The Vicar interrupted this flow with a gentle reminder of his question. He knew from experience that had he not done so then, within the hour, he would be fully acquainted with every single blemish in the optician's family history.

"Oh yes, now let me see. That's the quay and that there is thingy street...So that's the building on the corner.....So that one that's coloured in must be the old Harbour Office! It hasn't been used as that for a long time now mind you. After the Harbour Board moved further down the quay my grandfather, who was a builder, got the contract to do the alterations in there. He used to love going to the football every..."

"Thank you Mrs Fountain." Again the Vicar interrupted, this time more firmly. "Thank you very kindly, that was most helpful."

As the housekeeper returned to her duties a happier woman the Vicar resumed his study of the documents that he still did not fully understand. They seemed to allude to two buildings and yet only one was highlighted. It took him a full twenty minutes to discover that they referred to one building with two separate leases: one for the ground floor and the other for the first floor. This, he realised, was why his housekeepers football loving grandfather had been engaged to carry out alterations. The one building was now utilised as two separate entities. He could not help feeling that this information, spread over four virtually indecipherable paragraphs, could have been conveyed in one easily readable sentence. With a frown of annoyance he realised that, had this been the case, his coffee would not have gone cold before he had remembered to drink it. After a further thirty minutes of studying apparently nebulous phrases The Reverend Michael Grape experienced a life changing moment. This came with his sudden realisation that the upper rooms were leased to the Masters in the Prawning Fleet. The Vicar grinned at this discovery. Then he smiled, a smile which grew in intensity until it threatened to rupture his facial muscles. Leaping to his feet he found that he had a hitherto unknown talent for improvised dancing. He then felt very strongly that he wanted to locate his housekeeper and inform her that there was indeed a God in Heaven. Instead, deciding to share this message with the world, he ran from the Vicarage.

It took The Reverend Michael Grape just two minutes to get from the Vicarage to the Church. Once inside he made straight to the bell-ropes from where he proceeded to startle his Parish with a frenzy of unscheduled campanology. Despite the high volume that the mighty bells emitted from their belfry those passing by close to the Church would have heard his great voice crying out; "PRAISE THE LORD!"

Chapter Nine

Paradise had the usual collection of early evening drinkers in attendance as the dripping wet Boathook Bald entered. As was normal for this den of lawlessness, every voice within fell silent as soon as the door was opened. This abrupt end to a dozen conversations only lasted a few seconds however: just long enough for every head to turn and see who it was encroaching upon their territory. If it had been a male and a stranger he would be immediately met with a sea of scowling faces and, if he was perceptive enough, he would realise that this was merely an invitation to state his business - and this to be done with the minimum of delay! As on this occasion it was a familiar face the conversations were continued as swiftly as they had ceased.

The prawnman noted with satisfaction that a seat close to the roaring fireplace was free. It had been his hope that he would be able to dry himself in front of its blazing warmth whilst enjoying a quart of cider. This, his regular beverage for the early evening in Paradise, had started being poured by Dave Legg as soon as he saw the sodden prawnman enter.

"You been in the bastard sea again?"

Though Leggy phrased this as a question it was intended purely as a remark and Boathook Bald felt no need to reply, he being far too intent on making his way to the fireplace to secure for himself the vacant seat before another claimed it. His passage across the room was aided by those stood in his path quite willingly moving to allow him to pass, this not being out of generosity of spirit but more due to their reluctance to come in contact with the wet clothing. It was only once his objective had been successfully attained that the prawnman then turned his thoughts to Leggy's observation.

"Ah well, y'knows 'ow 'tis with these Masters," He said as the quart pot was placed on the table beside him, "they're lookin' after us. Makin' sure the boat don't get too much wear an' tear early on in the season. When all's said an' done, without the boat we's sunk!"

For a short while Boathook Bald contented himself with staring at the steam, already rising in swirls from his clothing in the fierce heat of the open fire. Wishing to partake of a smoke whilst enjoying his cider, he took his pipe and tobacco pouch from his pocket and put these in the grate to dry. All around him were conversations in full flow, creating a cacophony of indecipherable voices from which the occasional sentence would escape into the public domain. Some of the talk was in-depth as matters relating to the need to set the world to rights, though these topics tended to be discussed by those generally more familiar with the price of a pint of cider than with the complexity of global economies. But these debates were few in comparison to the exchanges between the local fishermen, their sparse use of language giving opinions regarding their work in a series of abrupt sentences;

"Any good out there?"
"Nah, rubbish!"
"We got a few."
"Tide's all wrong!"
"An' them easterlies don't 'elp."
"Balls, aint it?"

"Master wer'n't 'appy!"
"Bloody never is!"
"Good man though."
"I reckon."

And so it went on: sentences which had been uttered day in and day out since, it seemed, the beginning of time without their ever losing their validity. In an occupation (though they themselves regarded it as a calling) where earnings were subject to so many forces of nature before they could even consider the fickleness of the market place, the fishermen viewed their lot in life with an air of pessimistic acceptance. And though many of them claimed that they would 'get out o'the fishin' if I could' and do something else for a living, they knew that in doing so they would lose more than they gained: not in financial terms, it is true, but in the loss of their identity. To be a fisherman set them apart, it was their place in the world. They had their own language, their own hours and, more importantly, a secret store of knowledge which only they possessed. Where others would look out upon a stretch of sea and be aware only of a surging mass of water, dense and unfathomable, the fisherman could see more: he would have an intimate grasp of the unseen seabed, he would know its contours and of any features thereon which may obstruct his nets. And, if there were fish to be caught, he would know their hiding places. Such lore had been passed down through the fishing families and this wisdom became inbred into each successive generation. They came from a line reaching far back over the centuries, an ancestry which gives a nation its breed of sailors.

Closer to where Boathook Bald sat in his own private world of steaming cotton and invigorating cider the voice of John Scott dominated all. For John was a talker from the moment that he awoke each morning until the time he fell asleep each night: the man never kept quiet. When in Paradise this extrovert presence would regale all within earshot with stories his own rich and varied life: the places that he had visited, the things that he had done, men that he had fought and women that he had loved. He had sailed through storms the ferocity of which were unimaginable in order to land uncountable quantities of fish, the fortunes that he had won and lost in doing all of this he could shrug off as being of no account. Though all of his tales were sprouted from a seed of truth they were each a sapling which had grown in the telling until, though still vaguely credible, were hardly to be believed. Their credibility was further stretched by the fact that the regulars in this drinking den had heard him give many variations of the same story, occasionally more than once during an evening. An exotic Princess that he had almost married might on one occasion live in India and, in the next telling of the yarn, be several thousand miles away in China - depending entirely on the route that John Scott had taken before reaching that particular part of the story.

But fortunately for those who, willingly or otherwise, comprised John's audience the man had a beautiful speaking voice. Such was the perfection of its musical quality that it was possible to listen to him for hours if necessary (and it very often was) without wishing that he would shut up. This exceptionally comfortable timbre had nothing of the annoyance to be found in those whose voices had a distinct cutting edge, so much so that it was easily possible to allow the sound of his narratives to fade into the background. Sat within a few feet of the highly animated figure of John Scott this is exactly what Boathook Bald was now doing, his thoughts drifting back to the afternoon's work. In his opinion they had done very well: all three of last years lost pots had been recovered as well as one from the season before, this last having been given up as lost into deeper water. In addition to these four known to legitimately be the property of Master Miles, they found two which did not seem to belong to anyone. These were hurriedly concealed under some fish-boxes, lest one of the other Masters should attempt to hijack this act of providence by proving ownership of these strays.

"...So I've got this tooth at the front which broke a couple of years ago when Shirley found me in bed with three of her sisters and belted me in the face with a mop. The dentist gouged out the inside of it, stuck a little metal pin in and built up a new tooth around it..."

Normally such a good haul would have given Master Miles some pleasure but, to the contrary, as the afternoon wore on his temper had gone from bad to worse. Being the only crewman on board the *Prudence*, Boathook Bald had to bear the brunt of his Master's ill humours.

"...Jean and me had been trying to get each other in bed for years, she always fancied me like mad. Trouble was, her old man twigged it and kept warning me off. Luckily he eventually goes and gets himself drowned when he's fishing out of Scotland, went chasing the big money and copped a storm. Anyway, with him gone there was no holding us back..."

Once all of the pots had been safely stowed on board the *Prudence*, Master Miles had pointed out to Boathook Bald that there was something floating past the boat. As the crewman leaned over the side to take a look, he suddenly felt a pair of strong hands gripping his ankles. Within seconds he then found himself being pitched overboard.

"...Jean was going mad for me, couldn't wait to get me into bed! And with all the waiting we'd had to do I was pretty keen to finally taste the goods..."

"I am not in the business of carrying passengers." The Master had told him as he trod water beside the prawning vessel. "And as I have finished with you for the day, you can swim back."

"...so there we are quite happily splashing about between each other's legs when I suddenly notices that there's a gap where this tooth used to be..."

Pausing only long enough to remind the exhausted crewman that he was not to be late for work the following morning, Master Miles then fired up his small inboard engine and put his bow towards the harbour entrance. For the first time that day a slight smile appeared on the Admiral's lips as he left Boathook Bald to cover the five miles back the dock under his own steam.

"...I'm trying to find out where this bloody tooth has gone and hoping I can stick it back in before she notices. I've felt all around the sheet, but it aint there so that means there's only one other place it could've gone..."

It had taken him several hours but the effort had not been without its compensations, especially once he had met up with a few other crewmen also pitched overboard by their various Masters. Indeed, the natural camaraderie that existed between them created quite a holiday atmosphere as they partook of the arduous swim home.

"...and she suddenly decides that she wants me to kiss her and I know that if I do that then the game is up. Let her see me with a gap in my teeth and she'll go right off me! And not being able to find it is starting to stress me and then I suddenly had a daft thought: what if I do find a tooth here and it aint mine?..."

When the crewmen finally walked ashore at the Fisherman's Dock, Boathook Bald found his Master in a better frame of mind. Once the Admiral had got together with the other

Masters who had sent their crewman overboard that day, some lively wagering had taken place on the first of these worthies to make it back. As Boathook Bald had been the first to actually clear the water, Master Miles had profited very nicely from the afternoon's work. He was even heard to chuckle.

"...and she's starting to demand that I kiss her, says it'll make her feel good to have our lips together. So there's Jean getting all romantic and me getting even more worried about this tooth when, just as I'm running out of excuses to stay under the covers, I found it. Luckily the metal pin was still attached..."

The general rule in the Prawning Fleet was that whenever a Master was heard to make any sound closely resembling a laugh his crewman could relax. Despite having been kicked on the shin by one of the other Masters (who was known to take losing a wager with very bad grace) it was an extremely contented Boathook Bald who had made his way to Paradise to dry out in front of the fire.

"...so the tooth is back in place and I can concentrate on the job in hand. I'll tell you what, that woman swears blind that she don't believe in a God but she don't half start screaming and hollering at one when she comes!"

Suddenly the door flew open and, with a shrill demonic cackle, a figure jumped over the threshold and into Paradise. As the startled occupants of the room fell silent the man leapt up onto the centre table and began executing a crazed dance along its length. Reaching one end he would turn and repeat his steps as he made his way to the other, giving vent to the demonic cackle at irregular intervals as he did so. From his attained height above the heads of the drinkers, by now staring dumbfounded at this impromptu performance, the man's wild abandon seemed untameable and unending.

Until, that is, one of the whores threw an empty cider pot in the direction of the dancer, scoring a direct hit upon his skull;

"Fid! Will you behave yourself." she shouted at the man, one Fiddler Crabbe by name.

At this the dance came to an end amongst the cheers and jeers from the rest of the room. Ignoring any possibility of injury to his head from the cider pot, the man immediately sat upon the table with his feet resting on a bench. Facing the whore he took a fiddle from the case that he was carrying and, after placing the delicate instrument under his chin, bowed a few notes across its strings;

"Jane, Jane, Jane the Stain," he sang, "I been there afore an' I'm goin' back again."

"You aint goin' nowhere 'til I sees your money!" replied Jane in a voice, and with a look, which managed to convey both affection and commercial firmness in equal measures. "Now play that thing prop'ly or put it away."

Fiddler Crabbe laughed aloud before launching into a furiously paced reel upon the fiddle, his foot stamping on the bench keeping time with the music. The effect of this music upon the rest of the room seemed to send the occupants into a state of mass hypnosis. As individuals became one seething entity, conversations which moments before had held great importance were forgotten in an instant. With alcohol making them numb to pain they inflicted damage to each others ankles as jigs broke out in their midst, hands clapping in time to the tune sent elbows sharply into unaware ribcages. The only concern was that the music should not come to an end, so effective was it as a medium to momentarily dismiss the daily cares from their shoulders.

Sitting upon the table, the instigator of this transformation was oblivious to all. With eyes tightly closed he appeared to be the body being played by the instrument rather than its virtuoso. It was only his facial muscles that showed any sign that each note was being coaxed out of the great array of sheet music stored within his brain. Some bars of notes would be pushed out, here his upper body leaned into the fiddle and he appeared to be sneering at some unseen point in the middle distance. Yet other bars would flow out, almost without his bow touching upon the strings. With these he would lean back slightly, his eyebrows raised and his features relaxed suggesting that the sun was upon his face. Occasionally he would allow himself a smile of the kind that implies a private joke. Its meaning was clear: although the sight of his audience was hidden from his eyes he knew full well that his music had them under his control. They ate from his hand and, like so many Pavlov's Dogs, he could make them wait until the moment that he decided that they should dine. Thus, he controlled the tempo of the music to give them the high and low points which would serve to both excite and relax them by turns. By this same magic he brought the reel to a close at an optimum moment: not too soon to give disappointment to his listeners but in plenty of time to regain his breath from his exertions.

For a split second silence reigned before calls for another tune broke out amongst enthusiastic applause. Such was their pleasure that the majority of the audience even temporarily forgot that Fiddler Crabbe owed them money. But Dave Legg, placing a pot of cider at the musician's side, made it clear that the music was to cease - at least temporarily.

"Don't start drawing attention to the place this early on." he growled, "Wait 'til every bastard out there's asleep!"

And Fiddler Crabbe, who had only intended trotting out tunes until he was given a drink, was more than happy to comply with this order.

"Sorry Leggy," he said sheepishly, "I didn't 'ave the price of admission t'night. I 'ad t'get that first one in or I'd go dry."

With these words, placing the fiddle carefully back into its case, he blew a kiss to Jane the Stain and turned his attention to the pot of cider. His approach to this liquid was, for this first drink of the day, a carefully observed ritual for Fiddler Crabbe. The first three mouthfuls were partaken of in his own idiosyncratic manner; The first of these was a quick slurp: "T'get the taste of it." he would explain. The second would be a deeper draught, swallowed as soon as it entered his mouth: "T'wash the taste o'the day away." Whilst the third would be equally as deep but taken more slowly: "T'fully do justice t'Mother Nature's gift o'cider."

After fully savouring this mouthful he would gaze lovingly into the depths of the cloudy beverage in the pot.

"Look in there," he would sometimes say, "an' y'c'n see y'whole future mapped out f'r you."

Should a person overhearing him say this venture to ask him what this future held, Fiddler Crabbe without averting his gaze would sigh contentedly and reply;

"More o'this stuff! Lots more o'this stuff!"

Once the taste had been got, the day washed away and justice seen to be done, Fiddler allowed his eyes to wander around the room. During this appraisal of his surroundings the expression on his face suggested that he was seeing it for the first time since his arrival, which was indeed the case. Up to this point his sole intention had been to create a disturbance and, having arrested the attention of all, play music until he was given a drink. His purpose now in looking around at his fellow drinkers was twofold: firstly, he wanted to see if there was a likely direction from which his next drink would come. Though his pot was still near full this situation would soon change and, ever one to plan ahead in such matters, the musician liked to be prepared. The second reason for his reconnaissance was purely social: he was seeking an acquaintance in whose company he could enjoy conversation. As a rule he would be sure to get the latter but probably not the former, the attitude in Paradise tending to be ambivalent towards musicians. When an instrument was enlivening the atmosphere its master was treated with exceptional generosity. At such times Fiddler Crabbe, opening his eyes between tunes, would see an ever growing line of full cider pots on the table in front of him. But as soon as the music ceased it took with it the audiences' affection towards its creator.

"It mus' be me eyes they don't like," Fiddler would growl, "the bastards avoid 'em!"

And this was true. Whenever he looked around the room with an empty cider pot in his hand instead of his fiddle, all heads would turn away in order to better ignore his gaze.

"'ere we go, 'e's cadgin' pints again!" Would be muttered from the corners of mouths.

The best that a musician could hope for at these early evening times was either a visiting sailor, one with a deep purse and a wish to swap tunes, or one such as himself: a person with little but a willingness to share what he did have. When Fiddler Crabbe spotted Boathook Bald sat by the fire he knew that his immediate needs would be met, the prawnman being a friend whose pot would be divided amongst them both without question. But it was not only for the slating of thirsts which saw the musician now leaping to his feet.

"Baldy! Jus' the man, I needs t'ave a chat wi'you."

He grabbed his pot from the table and made his way to a

seat next to the rapidly drying Boathook Bald.

"Ol' Fid's been 'earing some talk," he continued as he made himself comfortable in front of the fire, "Master Miles aint an 'appy man, none o'the Prawnin' Masters are, an' I knows the reason why!"

"'ello Fid," replied the prawnman, "An' I reckon y'right, there were somethin' botherin' the Master t'day. Not that 'e's goin' t'tell the likes o'me an' quite right too. 'Know y'place an' keep it' is what my gran'father tol' me an' I aint never foun' no 'cause t'argue 'gainst it. Mind you, 'avin' said that, if somethin' is both'rin' Master Miles then Boat'ook Bald wants t'know 'bout it!"

By unspoken agreement the two men inclined their heads toward each other. Resting their elbows on the table they adopted low voices: the sort most suitable for discussing matters which were not, strictly speaking, their own business. Huddled thus in conference, shielding themselves from the ears of the rest of the room, Fiddler Crabbe enlightened his friend.

"As y'know Baldy, y'ol'mate Fid gets aroun' an' sometimes 'ears things that 'e aint by rights s'posed t'ear. Not that I goes pryin', not me! But y'can't 'elp over'earin' things when y'out there tryin' t'turn a shillin' or two..."

And in this way, all the time emphasising that he never willingly listened to things that did not concern him, he told of everything that there was to know about the approaching showdown between the Vicar and the Prawnmen. As he listened, occasionally interjecting with a question which always began with the words; "Now, o'course, this aint none o'my bus'ness. But..." Boathook Bald felt increasing alarm at what he was hearing. By the time all the facts had been laid bare his immediate response was one of passionate indignation.

"Well there may be as some who says that this don't concern me, but it do! If the Masters aint got their place on the quay then there aint no Stench. If there aint no Stench then there aint no hirin' for the fleet. An' if there aint no fleet then there aint no prawnin' an' we's all sunk without trace!"

To Boathook Bald the situation was this simple: he could not comprehend life carrying on without the structure being precisely as it had been for generations. At the top of this order stood the Masters, if they fell then everything, and everyone, below them would be swept away. The Club was something that he viewed as being necessary to the running of the fleet, without it he could only envisage a huge black hole with no Masters anywhere. This thought served to turn his indignation into determined action.

"Prawnin's gone on 'ere since time began an' I aint goin' t'stan' by an' let nobody stop it! That Vicar's bit off more'n 'e c'n chew if 'e thinks Boat'ook Bald is goin' t'let 'im get 'way with this. 'e's got t'be learnt t'stay in 'is Church an' not t'go 'bout upsettin' Master Miles!"

"Well spoke Baldy!" Fiddler slapped his friend upon the shoulder in admiration at these words, never before had he seen the prawnman roused to such a height of resolve. "What y'goin' t'do?"

The prawnman stared into the flickering embers of the fire as his mind juggled with possible solutions to the problem. After a minute or so he suddenly turned and looked the musician straight in the eye.

"Dunno," he stated simply, "I can't think o'nothin'."

"Well now, that's where y'ol'mate Fid c'n 'elp. I aint one t'bother 'imself with what the posh folks gets up to as y'know. An' I knows that y'aint the sort t'go 'roun'wond'rin' 'bout it neither - 'only judge y'own kind' as me ol' gran'mother used t'say. But ol' Fid 'ere learned somethin' 'bout that Vicar that 'e'd not want other folks t'know what was goin' on. 'e's bein' a bit naughty an' when folks like 'im does that they 'ave t'keep it a secret, as y'know."

"'ang on, afore y'tell me we should 'ave some top-ups." The prawnman turned and motioned to Leggy stood behind the bar, a quick 'thumbs up' gesture which was immediately understood, "An' these're on me. I'm 'avin' a bit o'luck this week 'cos of that bloke I been tellin' 'bout our traditions. 'e got me cider in this mornin' an' I 'ad t'rush off afore I got chance t'skull it all. Leggy stuck it back in the barrel, so I got few in t'night."

Once Dave Legg had finished replenishing the two cider pots set upon the table and retired out of earshot, Fiddler Crabbe was ready to share his secret knowledge. This concerned unseemly behaviour, which took place at regular intervals, between the Vicar and a certain Miss Simpson. This latter was an unremarkable woman of middle years who was a lifelong devoted member of the congregation. Known to have a rather haughty demeanour to all, even those of her own peer group, she was the very picture of respectability in her outward appearance. The Church was never afflicted with dust because Miss Simpson took it upon herself to remove every speck daily. At Harvest Festival time hers was the hand which decorated the Church with the Lord's blessings from the fields. She it was who laundered and ironed all cassocks and vestments, making perfect with needle and thread any minor repairs that were needed from time to time. In these and many other small ways she looked upon her position as a mainstay of the Church with devotion to duty. Given her reputation for severely criticising any whom she deemed to have strayed from the path of Godliness, it would have no doubt shocked many of her class to discover that she kept secret trysts with the Vicar.

These took place in the Church vestry at night and involved the sexual abandonment of both parties, this to the point that no depravity was held as taboo by the pair. Indeed, the fact that their congress was taking place on sacred ground, within the Church itself, gave the Vicar and Miss Simpson perverse delight. Fiddler Crabbe, in conveying this information, made his friend aware that this secret was known to himself and only one other person: the informant who had originally given this intelligence to the musician. Now that the prawnman had these facts in his possession, they could be used as the currency by which the Vicar's compliance could be bought. In short, if the matter of the lease was dealt with to the satisfaction of the Masters, then certain scandal would be avoided. Boathook Bald was delighted at the opportunity to save the Fleet which had been handed to him, though he did envisage one small problem to be overcome.

"Trouble is, I got t'find a way o'doin' it without causin' no upset t'this Miss Simpson. She aint done no upsettin' o'nobody an' it wouldn't be right t'get 'er involved!"

Despite this minor difficulty, the prawnman knew that he would now be able to deal with the Vicar. He raised his pot in salute to Fiddler Crabbe.

"We'll 'ave 'nother drink on account o'y'good fortune in findin' out 'bout this an' then we'll get Leggy t'fill up our pots an' drink some more!"

Leaning forward to the grate, the prawnman retrieved his pipe and inspected it closely. Satisfied that it was now dry enough to use he made a move to pick up his tobacco pouch but was halted by the musician.

"If all y'got in there is kerbstone twist, leave it be." instructed Fid, "I got some proper job 'baccy 'ere, I' got 'nough at the buskin' t'treat meself."

The two friends then proceeded to spend the rest of the evening toasting the saving of the prawning fleet for the benefit of future generations. Had they but known one vital piece of information they would have realised that their joy was misplaced: although Fiddler Crabbe had passed on the information regarding the Vicar and Miss Simpson in good faith, it was in fact a total fabrication. It was no more than a piece of scurrilous gossip invented by the person who had related it to the musician in the first place.

Chapter Ten

When Boathook Bald had received the message from Master Miles, telling him that they were to go and retrieve the lost pots, he had turned to the Visitor and apologised profusely.

"Sorry 'bout this, bloody knew this might 'appen, I got t'go out in the boat straight off. It goes like this sometimes an' it's a lot worse when cider gets wasted. But Master says now, so now it's got t'be!"

He looked regretfully into the pot, still nearly full despite the prawnman having taken several great slurps from its contents. For an instant the Visitor wondered where this apology was aimed: at himself or to the 'God–forgive-me', but before this thought could go any further the prawnman spoke again.

"Shame t'waste it." He nodded in the direction of the giant pot as he stood up and started to move away from the bench where it sat. In his mind he was unsure if this sudden curtailing of his conversation with the Visitor meant that the cider was now to be confiscated. It was, after all, his payment for talking that day. "An' y'might want t'finish it off y'self, seein' as 'ow y'paid f'r it. But watch out, if y'aint used t'good cider like this it c'n give y'the squits."

Boathook Bald backed away from the bench, his brain in turmoil: on one hand there was the wrath of Master Miles if his crewman delayed their work that day, on the other there was the question of the cider. The prawnman was unable to tear his eyes away from the pot, worried that the Visitor might wish to recover his investment or, worse still, that it would be left to go stale...

"So if y'aint goin' t'drink it y'self, take it back t'Leggy an' ask 'im t'pour it back in the barrel. Then I got some f'r when I gets back but that's only if y'aint goin' t'drink it. Y'c'n do that o'course 'cos it's yours, jus' s'long as it don't go t'waste."

The Visitor opened his mouth to reply, his intention being to inform Boathook Bald that he did not wish to drink the cider. Further, that he had no objection to taking the pot back into Paradise where it could await the prawnman's return that evening: but he was not given the chance to speak. Having reached a point some fifteen foot away from where the Visitor still sat, Boathook Bald suddenly ran back and picked up the 'God–forgive-me'.

"Tell y'what," he said, moving away again and clutching at the giant pot as if it were his dearest possession, "I'll take it an' give it t'Leggy m'self on the way past. It'll save on y'legs y'see. Anyways, y'won't want t'be drinkin' it y'self. See y't'morrow then."

Fearful that the Visitor may contradict this plan, and also aware that he should not keep Master Miles waiting, he turned and ran. During this escape he sidestepped briefly into Paradise to put the cider in safekeeping for his return later. When he emerged from the doorway his expression was one of great relief: whatever the rest of the day held in store for him he knew that he had a drink to look forward to at the end of it.

The Visitor watched him go without feeling too perturbed about his research being thus suddenly terminated. He felt the need for some breathing space, a feeling shared by many who sat near a prawnman for any length of time. As well as this, his enquiry about traditions involved with the painting of their vessels had brought forth a disappointing result. This subject was one that he had found quite fascinating in other fishing communities: what may, to the uninformed, appear to be the simple act of applying a final coat of paint was very often much more than this. The colour schemes were steeped in superstition and tradition, so much so that a fisherman would occasionally refuse to put to sea in a boat if the colour was not to his liking. Boathook Bald's only comment on the painting of prawning vessels however was terse and to the point.

"If the tin o'paint is goin' cheap then that's the colour the boat'll prob'ly be. An' if a tin o'paint is goin' f'r free then that's what colour the boat'll def'nat'ly be!"

The Visitor felt that it was time to read up on his notes, prepare an interim report, and then decide how much more time he should spend in this town. His company would have expected him to have finished here some days ago but, as he had contacted them to make them aware of his initial difficulties, they were happy to let him have more time: such was his record for excellent results that they knew this would be to their benefit. It has to be noted that, in this instance, their trust in him was misplaced for there was something other than professional interest keeping him here. It was not only the community that he was researching, though he did find them fascinating. They seemed to be stuck in a centuries old way of life which was almost still a feudal system, unheard of anywhere else these days. It was as if decades of social reform had completely passed them by, or had been strongly resisted even by those who would gain the most from them.

But more than this, it was here where he had first walked along a quay whilst wearing his father's uniform. This one act had served to make him feel part of this town in some small way and an inner voice was telling him to stay awhile. It was an instinct that he had developed over recent years: it was almost as if he could smell something in the air. Whether he was following a lead on part of his family's history or talking to the folk who were earning him his salary, he knew when a vital piece of information was imminent. Now, sat in the early afternoon sun, he could release his mind from work matters and concentrate on what this could be.

Despite the misunderstanding with Lucy Love he knew that his walk along the Town Quay had been significant: he had to do it again, in uniform, proudly. He certainly could not leave the town until he had done so, even though another inner voice was telling him that it was all a sham, a pretence, that he was only fooling himself. Little did he know that this small port had played a part in his family history, albeit in only minor ways. It was on this same quay where, some seventy years previously, his paternal grandparents had met one another for the very first time. He had just stepped ashore from his ship whilst she was visiting the town with her parents. Their initial attraction to each other soon blossomed into love and they were married within three years, but such details of their original courtship had never been known except to those two. The one other incident to involve this town concerned their eldest son - the Visitor's father. This too was a piece of family history which the Visitor would not find, no matter how diligent his research. As a very young sailor, just starting his career as an officer cadet, his father's ship had docked in this port. With his first ever taste of shore leave, and with his first pay packet, he also had found love: though his had been of the temporary kind that was paid for in a room above one of the quayside inns. Once more back at sea however, the subsequent joy at ridding himself of his virginity had very soon lost its lustre. In its place arrived his first encounter with a venereal disease, a condition diagnosed with great hilarity by the ship's doctor, who always found it amusing when the young salts went to him in the same sweat. Though the Visitor was not to know of these two events which gave him a connection to the town, some residue of his forefathers' presence remained. It would be only the most blinkered sceptic who could ever deny that some things are just meant to be.

Sitting in total unawareness of any possibility that those in the spirit world may, for better or for worse, be shaping the future by his being led to this town, he was joined by an elderly man who sat down beside him. Though smartly dressed, the stranger had the air of a retired manual worker rather than a more affluent member of the community. This impression was strengthened when he spoke, there clearly having been no attempts by himself or others to suppress his local accent.

"'ow do." the man greeted the Visitor, placing his walking stick beside him on the bench. "Me name's Frank, but all me mates calls me 'Bilge-pump'"

"Oh, er, how do you do, er, Bilge-pump."

"Now then," the man spoke firmly but without any anger, "Don't y'go callin' me that! Only me mates calls me that."

"I do beg your pardon Frank." the Visitor was at pains to make amends and this showed in the sincerity with which the apology was given.

"Buggers! They knows I don't like 'em callin' me that! Y'aint from roun' 'ere, are you."

This last was clearly not a question, it was a statement. Nevertheless, purely as a social nicety, the Visitor treated it as the former.

"No, actually I'm from..." which is as far as he was allowed to go before the old man commandeered the conversation once again.

"I knew it! Y'don't smell like y'come from 'roun' 'ere. I bet y'never smelt a town like this one afore, 'ave you?"

"Well, now you come to mention it, I don't think I have."

"An' I'll tell y'why young man. This town smells of an 'onest day's work! If y'go 'alf a mile that way," here Frank grabbed his walking stick and used it to indicate a direction to the north of where they sat, "Over there y'gets the smell o'the grain silos. When a wind brings their smell 'cross the town y'c'n 'ardly breath sometimes."

"Dreadful!" the Visitor could only remark, "They should do something about it!"

"Why?" the old man leapt to the aroma's defence, "It's an 'onest smell, it's the smell o'work, the smell o'folks makin' a livin'!"

Once again using his walking stick Frank pointed to the east. "Over that way used t'be the gasworks, an' that was a whiff if ever I smelt one! Dirty filthy place it was. It's twenty year or more since they pulled the place down, but there aint one 'mongst those who r'member it that wouldn't wish it back."

During this discourse Frank had become increasingly agitated, his walking stick being used both as a direction indicator and as a means of showing the universe that things were not to his liking. But of a sudden his shaking of the stick ceased: with it came a relaxing of his posture, a slumping of his shoulders, signs that he had long given up any serious expectations of the world he knew returning. When he spoke again it was with the tone of one who had spent many hours in reflection.

"Trouble is, they takes all these smells away from us with

no thought 'bout what they goin' t'r'place 'em with."

He turned to face east again: the direction to which he had spoken of so enthusiastically when talking about the gasworks now only earned his contempt.

"If y'walked over t'the ol' gasworks site now, y'wouldn't be able t'say what it smelt of. There's cars an' 'ouses an' shops-all sorts an' no smell t'any of 'em! What does it smell like where y'come from then?"

This question came unexpectedly and its arrival, accompanied by a sharp look from the old man's piercing blue eyes, caused the Visitor to stammer his reply.

"I...er....well...that is to say, I've never really thought about it."

"That's sad." said the old man. Then, pointing toward Paradise, he asked, "Y'ever been down there?"

Associating the street with its pungent aromas, the Visitor involuntarily wrinkled his nose in disgust at the thought of them. This reaction caused Frank to once again become highly defensive.

"Don't y'go pullin' faces like that young man, there's nothin' wrong with a place 'avin' its' own smell!"

"But," the Visitor replied, "It's just so bad."

"An' s'pose y'jus' tell me 'ow a smell c'n be bad?" Frank demanded, "Y'may not like it y'self but t'me the place smells warm an' comf'rtin', it tells me all's well with the world. 'ave y'ever been married young man?"

This change of direction in the conversation once again caught the Visitor unaware. Before he had time to think of the answer to this question the old man, correctly divining that hesitation implied a negative, carried on speaking.

"I'd rec'mend it t'any man! Not that it's always an easy ride 'cos it aint, far from it. No matter 'ow much I brought 'ome on pay day it was never enough. An' she told me so!

An' 'ouse proud! Y'can't b'lieve 'ow many 'idden dangers there are f'r a man walkin' 'roun' in 'is own 'ome."

At this point a far off memory gave its owner cause to smile and he was silent for a while. Then, just when he appeared to be about to share this thought with the Visitor, another memory seemed to overtake him and his mouth clamped shut again. When he did finally resume speaking it was in the tone of one who had not lost the ability to mourn.

"She died seven year ago." he said with a sigh, "An' I still misses 'er ev'ry day. We 'ad good times an' bad times, same as ev'ry one else, but there was never a day when I didn't want 'er there b'side me. We was a team an' a good one too!"

Following these revelations there was a pause as Frank held his feelings in check. The Visitor, never one to be able to deal with his own emotions let alone those of a complete stranger, felt awkward. Despite this, he did find himself warming to the old man. It may have been an empathy for another who had suddenly found himself alone in the world, or it may have been the Visitor's curiosity in learning about the lives of others. Whatever the reason, the Visitor wanted to hear more: he did not have long to wait.

"An' d'y'know what binds a couple so close t'gether? Y'don't an' so I'll tell you. It's their smell!

When I come in from work ev'ry day she'd always know what sort o'day I'd 'ad an' I knew all 'bout 'ers - it was all down t'smell. Same went for when one of us was ill or upset or worryin'. It's all there in a person's smell an' after years of bein' wed it's somethin' y'can't 'ide. O'course mos' o'the time it's jus' the smell o'famil'arity, even if it's jus' the pong o'the kippers y'both 'ad for breakfas'. It's what y'looks forward to in each other, bein' able t'smell that all's well in the 'ome. See them seagulls over there? Them's the mos' dang'rous birds in the world! I knows that for a fact, an' don't y'go lettin' anyone tell y'otherwise young man."

This latest example of Frank's tendency to shift his line of thought without warning made the Visitor wonder what the gulls had to do with marriage. Momentarily he felt a dizziness as his brain tried to make the two subjects compatible with each other before another part of his brain, the area that deals with short term memory, reminded him of Frank's idiosyncrasy. Thus reassured, his tongue was able to form a reply.

"Really?" the Visitor expressed surprise at this assertion, "I always thought they were fairly stupid creatures."

"They are, most o'them. It's the ones that aint stupid that're dang'rous." Frank said with spirit. "Them birds c'n live t'be 'bout thirty year old but mos' of 'em, the stupid ones, are lucky t'see five. Now then, the ones what do live longer'n five year are the clever ones. Them's the birds that've learned 'ow t'survive y'see an' they gets their full lifespan on that 'count."

"How fascinating, I never knew that. So why does this make them more dangerous?" asked the Visitor, his curiosity only matched by his disbelief.

"See them ones over there followin' that boat in?" again the walking stick was being used as an indicator, this time in the direction of a vessel heading up between the quays. "They knows they c'n get a feed out o'that boat, it's a fishin' boat an' there'll be lots o'scraps o'fish on it for 'em. Now that aint partic'ly clever, all the seabirds knows 'bout that. When I was out there fishin' them ones didn't bother me at all. The ones t'look out for is the ones that don't only follow y'boat in, they follows y'ome as well. Them's the dang'rous buggers!"

"They used to follow you home?" the Visitor tried to give

curiosity precedence over disbelief as he spoke these words. It had not been an easy task, but Frank was by now too immersed in his diatribe to notice if there was any doubt showing in the Visitor's tone.

"Worse than that!" the old man looked into his past and glumly recalled great injuries done, "One of the basta'ds got so clever 'e worked out 'ow t'break into me 'ouse! Ate all me dinner an' then shat all over the place 'e did. I shouted an' swore at 'im an' 'e jus' flies up on a roof an' laughs at me. Y'mark my words, one day them birds'll 'ave us all out o'our 'omes an' take over the town. Would y'like t'see me false leg young man? Nowadays they makes them out o'all sorts o'new-fangled mater'als, but I've 'ad this one f'r forty year. Made out o'wicker it is an' it's done me proud all that time. Quack says I c'n 'ave plastic one whenever I wants. 'No thanks' I says to 'im, 'this leg'll do me out, an' the next poor bugger that 'as t'use it too'!"

As Frank suddenly bent his arms forward to roll up his left trouser leg in order to display his pride and joy, the Visitor's mind was made up: he would stay in this town longer, he wanted to meet more of its folk. Another week, he told himself, at least another week. He had some holiday from work due to him and a holiday it would be: he would put his notebook away. It was, he felt, time that he started meeting people for who they were rather than for what they could supply to his company. Though he could not fully comprehend it, the chance meeting with Frank had made him aware of how alone he was in his life. It was not the allusion to his marital status which had caused this, a close relationship had never featured in his life nor had he ever considered the possibility. It was not a case of not wanting one, more due to the fact that it had simply never happened. But now he felt the onset of a discontent with his life: a life which to date had entailed him meeting many hundreds of people and yet not getting to know any of them. Taking his leave of Frank with a warm handshake, the Visitor set off to contact his office to let them know of his plans. He would forward his interim report to them the following morning. On an impulse when passing Paradise he walked in and handed a five pound note to Dave Legg: this, he instructed, was to be converted into cider for Boathook Bald when he returned from his work. As he made his way out of Paradise the Visitor was not sure why he had done this, but he was aware that this spontaneous act of largesse had made him feel good. This was the start of a series of events which would ensure that by the time he left this town the Visitor was to receive an important lesson, an experience which would change his outlook forever.

At eight o'clock that evening, as Boathook Bald and Fiddler Crabbe enjoyed sharing in the Visitor's generosity and plotted the downfall of the Vicar, The Masters met at The Club. Fourteen very sombre figures sat around the table looking towards Master Miles. Their Admiral, by tradition, was seated at the eastern end of this solid oak furnishing and, for the moment, was holding his own counsel. The seat facing him from the western end of the table was always kept empty: this was so to represent to the Masters the void that would exist without their brotherhood. The symbology behind this arrangement was plain. In the east the sun rises and gives light, while in the west it sets bringing only darkness. It has to be said that this outward display of unity, an almost Masonic set of secret rules and rituals, which seemingly bound the Prawning Masters to each other was extremely superficial. As a matter of honour, not one single man sat around that table would miss an opportunity to steal from, or cheat, a fellow Master if there was the slightest chance of doing so. The one exception to this was their acknowledged Admiral: he was held to be above such behaviour and respected accordingly.

The present mood which pervaded the room had not been improved by the fact that, as they each arrived at The Club, the Vicar had made sure that he was standing outside of the building. No words were bandied between The Reverend Michael Grape and any of the Masters, but none were needed. The looks which they had exchanged spoke volumes, the Vicar making his joy at an anticipated victory known to every single one of them. For the most part the Masters tried to act nonchalant: they wished to give the impression that their business that evening was a mere trifle, of little or no consequence whatsoever. But in reality all knew that a battle would soon ensue and all involved were aware of who held the advantage of wind and tide. Not content with making his gloating presence felt upon their arrival, this one-man paramilitary wing of the Onward Christian Soldiers (as one of the Masters had humourlessly dubbed the Vicar) was stood outside still. They could not see him from their first floor windows but the prawnmen were aware of his proximity to themselves. The windows were open to the evening breeze and he could be heard, sometimes allowing himself an excited chuckle and occasionally clapping his hands as he broke into a short dance.

It was this latter sound which finally galvanised Master Miles into action. Though he, as yet, had no constructive thoughts on a solution to their problem, he knew that nothing could be discussed whilst the Vicar was within earshot. He reached across the table and rang the small hand-bell which was used to summon Sweaty Betty into the room.

"Ah Betty," he said upon her arrival, "would you be so kind as to fetch a bucket of slops from your kitchen. I would like you to tip them out of the window and onto the head of the Vicar, if you please."

With a grin which suggested that the passing of the years had not quelled a tomboy within, Sweaty Betty performed this task enthusiastically and with great accuracy. A murmur of approval, coupled with the nodding of fourteen heads, showed that the assembled prawnmen favoured their Admiral's opening salvo. The 'well dones' and the 'bravos' were quickly drowned out by the massive bellow of rage from the street outside. Following this The Reverend Michael Grape was heard to withdraw from the fray, though not without sending many threats in the direction of the open window. Despite the general feeling among the gathering inside that this had been a highly satisfactory tactic, all of them were aware that this had been no more than a skirmish: the main battle had yet to be enjoined.

It was to this main battle that they now turned their attention: long into the night the Masters discussed the dilemma facing them. On two things they were all agreed: something had to be done and, at the moment, none of them knew what that something was. To relocate The Club to an alternative venue was a possibility that not one of them would even suggest. It was unthinkable, a point of principle. Each and every one of them at one time during the evening mentioned that their father and their father's father had sat in this very room and this led to much talk of these revered ancestors turning in their graves. It was also noted, loudly and with great indignation, that the Masters were all men who were local to the town: born and bred, man and boy.

The Vicar was an outsider and who was he to come here and dictate what they could or could not do? After all these hours of discussion, however, they found themselves no closer to a solution than when they had started. The only positive move had come when Master Miles, fuelled by an alcohol driven determination, leaned from the window and ran up the Skull and Crossbones on the flagpole. This short fixture, set at a forty-five degree angle two thirds of the way up the front wall of the building, normally bore a Red Ensign. For the next week, the remaining time until the lease was due to be signed, the black flag would stay in place. War had now officially been declared: Master Miles knew that, as Admiral, he would have to lead his Fleet to a decisive victory.

~~*~~

Whilst the Masters in the Prawning Fleet were thus noisily engaged the Visitor, by comparison, was sat in his room concentrating his mind on silence. Silence and stealth: it was not how he would have chosen it to be for his second walk along the Town Quay in his father's uniform. He preferred to envisage himself being seen and recognised for the ship's Captain which he felt that he was, part of his family's heritage. Unfortunately, the confidence that he held inside regarding his right to be in uniform did not extend outside of this small boundary. The threat of being challenged and, worse, exposed as a fraudster meant that he would have to take his walk in the dark. Hopefully nobody would be around to see him and to issue such a challenge.

He had been sat in the room he occupied in the lodging house for an hour trying to read a magazine. His original intention had been to wait until Mrs Cousins had retired to bed for the night, then allow a reasonable time to elapse to ensure that she was asleep. At this point he would then change into the uniform, slip quietly out of the house and set off for his walk. This plan had altered slightly due to his impatience in carrying it out: unable to focus on anything to distract himself whilst waiting, such as reading the magazine, he had donned the uniform earlier. At first this had seemed like a good idea to him, the simple act of climbing into his father's clothes having its usual positive effect on his self-esteem. But he very quickly discovered that it had only served to increase his impatience and he was annoyed with himself for not having foreseen this. He was now overcome with the need for movement: in order to be that ship's Captain, that man of command, he needed to be away from his small lodging and within sight and sound of the sea. It was in his blood! Thus he had sat in his room with legs that were uncomfortable, fidgeting at their need to be walking. He kept shifting his position in the armchair to try and find a posture that would relax these limbs, but to no avail. All this time he was listening carefully for the sounds that Mrs Cousins made as she performed her nightly banalities. He was sure that on this evening she was taking longer than usual in her routine and this was causing him unreasonable vexations, so much so that he experienced uncharacteristic anger at the length of time it took for a cup of malted milk to be prepared and then consumed: did she really have to sip at it rather than take generous mouthfuls? And then there was the cat. By the time that Mrs Cousins was calling to the feline and gently coaxing it to go out for the night, the Visitor was close to exploding with frustration. He positively wished that he could just run downstairs, grab the creature by the scruff of its neck and throw it out of the house. Just to speed things along. Knowing that such feelings were extreme, he set his hands gripping tightly on the armrests of the chair instead of on the cat. And waited.

At long last the house was quietened. Mrs Cousins had been in her bed for a good half hour, and snoring audibly for twenty-five minutes, when the time finally came that the Visitor felt sure that he could make his way out of the house without disturbing her slumbers. To be on the safe side he moved around his room for a minute, all the time listening for any variation in his landlady's breathing. There was none. Encouraged, he then tiptoed very carefully from his room, all the time alert for a break in the sound of snoring and this caution he maintained as he slowly crept down the stairs and out through the front door. Closing this quietly, and congratulating himself on his success at getting this far, he stepped briskly down the street toward the Town Quay.

In the large front bedroom of the house which he had just vacated Mrs Cousins half awoke from a deep slumber. She briefly wondered why her lodger was creeping around at one o'clock in the morning dressed as a Merchant Navy Officer. Then, yawning toothlessly, she turned over and immediately fell back into a blissful state of slumber.

The short walk from the lodging house to the quay passed in quiet and solitude for the Visitor. So much so that the noise which he suddenly encountered at the end of the street made Lucy's brave captain freeze. In a heart thumping panic, and half prepared to turn tail and run back to his room, he stood listening intently for its source. He quickly relaxed when he realised that he had nothing to worry about: the noise was a combination of the drunken conversations emanating from two buildings, one to his right and the other to his left. The former was The Ship's Captains Reading Rooms from which came a constant loud murmur. The sound was quite unmistakenly the outcry of a small group of men who had a lot to say indignantly. The latter was Paradise in full swing but with the sound contained behind heavy wooden shutters. From this direction the steady babble of raised voices was punctuated by the sound of a fiddle and the occasional drunken screech. Edging forward cautiously the Visitor looked up and down the quay: it was deserted. Smiling broadly as his trepidation gave way to childlike excitement and pulling himself up to his full height, he took a moment to ensure that his uniform was straight. Satisfied with his appearance he then, adopting what the director of a pantomime would describe as 'a nautical gait', set off for his walk along the waterfront.

However, where one person might see a deserted quay another, more used to the architecture of such places, might see a different, less lonely, scene. This was due to Paradise, whilst providing ample opportunity for the imbibing of unlimited amounts of liquid, lacked any facilities for the body to dispose of the surplus generated. As a consequence of this, customers feeling the urge to relieve themselves had to find a place to do this outside of the building and the closest convenient spot was a part of the quay known as Ferry Steps. These steps were set into the edge of the quay, their original purpose being to serve as a landing point for the small rowing boats which would convey passengers between the quays. A man standing on one of the lower steps, using the wall in front of him as a urinal, would have his chin at ground level. Thus, he had a full view of anyone who should pass in front of his eyes yet with very little chance of his presence there being noticed. So it happened that as the Visitor set off to enjoy the salt air he was watched from the Ferry Steps by Derek Lipton. In spite of his drunken state Derek, the eldest of the Lipton Boys, made a mental note that here was a sailor, an Officer even, previously unknown to the family. This could be a useful piece of luck, Derek told himself, Captain Coates will be in port soon and looking for a crew for his ship.

This Captain Coates was one of the very few reasons that the Liptons now ever had the chance to practice as boarders. Their family had a proud history in this line of work but, by this time, there was very little need for this service: various pieces of legislation which had come into force over the years had rendered the demand virtually obsolete. These Acts of Parliament set out to ensure that conditions on board ships were now strictly monitored, subsequently common sailors had greater protection from rogue captains or shipping companies. For the most part these Acts, with a government department actively working to enforce them, achieved that which they set out to do. But there are loopholes in even the soundest of laws and a captain determined to exploit them would always manage to do so. For how long they could escape the notice of the authorities varied in each individual case, but the profits to be gained from malpractice made even short term breaches a worthwhile risk. Having said that, Captain Coates was an exceptional case, seemingly being able to flout the law with impunity. Some, and these tended to be those with never a good word to say about anybody, muttered accusations of corruption in high places: the implication being that certain officials were being paid to turn a blind eye to the Joan. Yet others, those with a less jaundiced view of the world, claimed that it was the captain's complete brazenness which allowed him to run his ship in such a way. The truth is that Captain Coates, for all his open show of defiance to the law, always covered his own back: if a complaint was ever to be levelled against him he would have a defence that would cast sufficient doubt upon his guilt. Let the sailors claim that they were forced into work on board his ship, he could counter with the accusation that they were merely mutinous dogs who plotted to cause mischief for their own ends! The Lipton Brothers, as part of their service, would always find witnesses to confirm that the crew had signed on to the *'Joan'* willingly.

With boarding as a full-time occupation no longer a viable option, the Lipton Boys now looked elsewhere for their main source of income. Their specialities were in areas which required a lot of physical strength coupled with very little in the way of brain power. This is not to say they were dullards, far from it, they just preferred not to have to waste time in thinking about their work because thought took time and time was money. Thus, they were much sought after by nightclub owners needing doormen, crooks needing favours called in, slum landlords with tenants that they wished to evict illegally and property developers with buildings that they wanted demolished. If something needed breaking, be it bones or brickwork, it was a job for the Lipton Boys. But when the opportunity to perform the office of boarder did present itself they approached the work with a different attitude: this was out of necessity. Boarding required careful planning and timing was of the utmost importance as a ship would only be in port for a couple of days at the most. During this time unwitting victims would have to be selected and then coaxed, or tricked, into being at the right place at the right time to be shanghaied. Unconsciousness had to last approximately twelve hours for the sailors chosen as the bare bones of this trade. Any less than this meant that they may still be within sight of land when they awoke and inclined to jump overboard in a bid for freedom. Longer than the twelve hours could be due to an excess of the knock-out drops which had been administered to them in the boarding house: an overdose of this toxin could render a man incapable of performing his duties for the duration of the voyage. It was the skill of the boarder to estimate the correct dosage for a victim's height and build, then to make sure that he received it at the optimum moment. The work would be more difficult when a known rogue ship was due in port: at these times most of the boarders' potential targets would be aware of this and, therefore, taking more care over their own personal safety. The landlords of the quayside inns would see a drastic fall in sales at these times as the sailors, the bulk of their customers, would make themselves scarce for a few days until the danger had passed. Despite this, the Liptons never failed to supply a ship with a crew when asked to do so. They had their family reputation to consider: generations of Liptons had proudly turned boarding into an art and the brothers saw themselves as craftsmen.

The imminent arrival of the *Joan* held much promise for these land sharks turned artisans: the captain had sent word that he would need an officer and four crewmen upon his departure. This could be interpreted as fat profit and adrenaline filled pleasure for the Lipton Boys. They were not in the least surprised at the number of crewmen required, which was a full ship's compliment for a vessel the size of the *Joan*. The hands that were on board when she arrived in port would waste no time in jumping ship: Captain Coates would have ensured that the food and conditions they had been subjected to were such that, as soon as the last mooring rope had been made fast, they would be gone. The alternative for these unfortunate souls was the danger of being shanghaied for another trip if the boarders got to them before they made good their escape, and of this they were fully aware. This expedient departure would also mean that they would not sign off for the voyage which they had just completed: therefore they would not receive what little payment they were due. But this was a price that anyone who found themselves serving on the *Joan* would pay in order to avoid a second trip. The financial advantages of this situation to Captain Coates meant that his ship had been crewed in this manner for many years.

The call for an officer was unusual: the rouge Captain knew that it was prudent to keep at least one such on board and to treat him with respect. In return he would have a man who could handle the ship when the captain slept and who would also keep the crew too busy to turn surly and, thereafter, careless in their work. For the last eight years Captain Coates had employed an officer who he could trust implicitly, a first mate whom he also looked upon as a good friend. The man's loyalty, and complicity, had been rewarded well in financial terms and he had been indispensable to the smooth running of the *Joan*. It was, therefore, more than a little inconvenient when the fellow fell overboard and got himself drowned during a storm on this present voyage. Until he could engage another mate who could be given the same level of trust, Captain Coates could only hope for the Lipton Boys to find him one capable of performing the duties required. This, he knew, was not going to be easy for the brothers to do: such men, having worked hard to gain their qualifications and a better lifestyle, were not so thick upon the ground in the quayside inns as common sailors. Hence Derek Lipton's interest in the Visitor's night time promenade in the uniform of an Officer of the Merchant Navy.

There was no way that the brothers could know of the Visitor's wish to follow in his family's maritime tradition. But, as fate would have it, it would be their plotting which stood to turn his wish into a reality. Even as he was buttoning up his fly, Derek Lipton was formulating a plan to get the Visitor into their boarding house and thence onto the *Joan.*

Chapter Eleven

Master Miles sat in the Morning Room considering his options, such as they were at that present time. That no immediate answer to his problem had presented itself as yet was causing him to focus too much on a negative outcome: this he knew was not helping the situation. He had to find a way of doing something, anything, to start the ball rolling - to create a chain of events which he could manipulate in order to bring them to a satisfactory conclusion. Satisfactory, that is, to the Masters in the Prawning Fleet. Whilst he sat thus one of his housemaids was gently coaxing his long dark hair into a ponytail. As her employer was obviously preoccupied with his own thoughts the girl did not want to interrupt his musings: rather than ask him which ribbon he wished to wear that day she chose, then deftly tied, a broad black bow to hold his hair tight to the nape of his neck. As she then stood back to inspect her handiwork she heard the Master speak but, so quiet had been his tone, that she did not hear what he said:

"I beg your pardon Sir?" she asked.

"Oh! I'm sorry Hilda," Master Miles turned to look at her, his expression suggesting that, until the moment she spoke, he had not even been aware of her presence in the room, "I was just thinking aloud really. I was wondering who would rid me of this turbulent priest."

His line of thought broken, the Admiral realised that nothing was going to get done by his sitting still and pondering: he needed to take action. Seeing him stand, and aware of what he would require next, Hilda took his jacket from its hanger and held it ready for him to slide his arms into the sleeves with the minimum of effort. As he did so, he glanced at his reflection in the full length mirror: the image of a proud Admiral in the Prawning Fleet gave him heart, he would win this battle! He allowed himself a few more seconds with his reflection whilst Hilda, her duties in aiding the Master in his toiletries now complete, withdrew from the room with a curtsy. As she did so, Master Miles crossed the room to gaze out of the window, his mind very much upon the advice which he had been given the previous day. This had been sound counsel but, as yet, there was no clear way in which he could see how it could be applied to the situation.

He had taken a copy of the lease to show a solicitor, a man who was also to be counted amongst his trusted friends. Master Miles had hoped that a practised eye would be able to discover a loophole in the legal jargon, a means whereby the need for the Church's involvement in the matter could be bypassed. Over genial pints of beer in one of the town's hostelries the solicitor studied the document at length. As he was thus engaged his facial expressions - a frown here, pursed lips there - showed that the person who had drawn up the lease had done so in such a way as to make it watertight: the Church's wishes could not be denied. When, at long last and with a shake of his head, he gave his advice it was strictly off the record.

"Have you thought about having this man bumped off?" he asked, in such a manner as to show that the suggestion was being made very much tongue in cheek.

This, in his wildest desperation, the Admiral certainly had. But, he had to acknowledge, this was too drastic a course of action. It was middle of the night thinking, the kind of madness which evaporated in the cold light of dawn when reason prevailed.

"I wouldn't wish the man harm," he had replied, "well, certainly not that much harm. Diarrhoea perhaps. Nothing worse than that though."

"In that case, you need to investigate his past," the solicitor pointed out, "There will be something there with which you can blackmail him. Find it, use it and the lease is yours. But keep your methods subtle, once you have your lever apply it gently. When the Reverend Michael Grape realises that you have the dirt on him, it will be sufficient to put the frighteners on. That is all it will take without you having to put yourself at risk by threatening him with exposure. Do that my friend and you may well end up in prison."

That there may be an embarrassment to discover in the Vicar's past was something which Master Miles doubted: he let scepticism be known.

"He's a man of the cloth through and through as far as I can see, he's going to be spotless."

"Don't you believe it!" was the expert's considered opinion, "I've spent enough time listening to legal evidence to the contrary! Oh I don't mean with men of the cloth in particular, but with pillars of the community in general. The fact that a person has such a standing makes it easier to bring them down - they are not exactly a Tom, Dick or Harry who care not what other people may think of them. I personally have won many a case not on the facts as they are, but on the unspoken implication that things may not be as they seem. It's the spotless ones, the upright bastions of society, who have ensured that I can afford to drive a Porsche!"

The solicitor friend of Master Miles paused to take a long sip at the beer. This fine brew was the only payment that he expected to receive for his legal expertise from the Admiral: that and, possibly, a few bags of prawns. He then relaxed back into his seat before continuing;

"Besides, such people are riddled with guilt over any minor infringement they may have committed in regard to their own moral code. This fear makes them believe they have done wrong even when they have not. Think about it."

So the Admiral had thought about it and was thinking about it still. The solicitor's words had rung true but, as yet, they had not brought the solution any closer. He stared out of the window where, for the want of anything else to focus upon, he watched two pigeons as they performed a courtship ritual on a nearby roof. It was a small, private, but fascinating spectacle to behold: the male bird had alighted upon the roof close a female that he wished to impress for the purpose of fornication. The female bird, fully aware of his intentions (and not completely averse to the idea of the aforementioned fornication) nevertheless turned her back on him, her manner suggesting that the fertilisation of her eggs was the last thing on her mind at that particular moment. This caused the male to embark upon a courtship dance. He circled on the spot, his head and neck made more prominent by the ruffling of the surrounding feathers. As he circled he also dipped his head up and down, causing the whole length of his body to see-saw in a most comical fashion. After a few minutes of this display the female seemed to get bored with the idea: she flew away to another roof nearby, knowing full well that the male would follow. This he did and the whole ritual started again.

Living in a place where pigeons proliferated this sight was not new to Master Miles. Having seen this courtship dance performed many times his fascination had, by now, been tinged with more than a little detachment. Today, however, the birds had provided him with a much needed distraction: for a few minutes his mind had been clear of the tumbling thoughts which only served to get in each others way. Subsequently, when he ceased gazing at the rooftops opposite and looked at the street below, he started to form a plan in his mind, a means whereby he could obtain information on the Vicar. It was the sight of a man making his way along the pavement which gave Master Miles his inspiration, an unassuming man known throughout the town as being the choirmaster. And so it was that the Admiral sent a message to a certain Jack Hatchard briefly informing him that his services were required.

Some eight hours later, and not for the first time in this story, the choirmaster found himself being held up against a wall. This time his throat was in the less ecclesiastical, but no less vice-like, grip of Jack Hatchard. Jack was of a large build and, at six foot one inch tall, two inches taller than the Vicar: if the choirmaster noticed that, therefore, his feet were two inches further above the ground than they had been the last time he had been held against a wall, he did not mention it. He was too engrossed in being terrified of Jack Hatchard, a man proud of his ability to frighten other folk with threats of violence. This was not something that he ever did for no reason (nor, indeed, for no pay) but when he was given the opportunity to practice this skill he liked to think that he was making a good job of it. For this reason the waylaying of his victim had been accompanied by much snarling and fist waving before the purpose of it was stated: namely, that the choirmaster had to provide him with details of the Vicar's past history.

"But...why?" gasped the choirmaster once he had been acquainted with the reason for Jack Hatchard's interest in him.

"Why!?" Jack's expression showed that not only did he consider this to be a foolish question, it was also one which he did not expect to be asked. "Because if you don't give me the information I will smack you in the mouth. That's why!"

"But if the Vicar finds out, he will probably smack me in the mouth." said the choirmaster miserably. These words turned out to be precisely the wrong ones to direct at Jack Hatchard: his grip on the choirmaster's throat became a little tighter and his snarling became more intense.

"Are you trying to say that this Vicar bloke is better at smacking people in the mouth than I am?" He clearly felt wounded by the idea that somebody may even think such a thing.

"No! No! I am not saying that at all!" came the reply in the terrified tones of one aware that his situation was becoming more critical by the minute.

"So you are saying that you'd rather get smacked in the mouth by the Vicar than by me?" Jack was starting to get very angry.

"No, no, no," the choirmaster was close to tears of despair, "I do not want to be smacked in the mouth by anyone. And I do not know what I can tell you about the Vicar, he is a very private man. Nobody here knows much about his past, only a few details which were in a letter sent just before he arrived to take up his post."

Jack Hatchard released the grip on his hapless victim's throat. Having had the choirmaster's position in the affair explained more fully he was at pains to point out that the situation need not be so complicated. The Admiral's instruction had been for any piece of information, no matter how small.

"Look," he said carefully, "You get that letter and give it

to me tomorrow without the Vicar finding out. Then nobody gets smacked in the mouth by nobody, see?"

He let loose his hold on the choirmaster who, thinking that his immediate ordeal was over, allowed himself a silent sigh of relief. This turned out to be premature however as Jack was struck by a new thought;

"I know!" he shouted, causing his reluctant co-conspirator to cower in renewed terror, "If the Vicar threatens to smack you in the mouth, tell him that I'll smack him in the mouth! I'll see you tomorrow then."

And, satisfied that he had now sorted out all problems satisfactorily, Jack Hatchard left the choirmaster to deal with his part of the bargain.

Hitherto the choirmaster had been a lifelong devotee of mild manners: 'By Jove!' being the strongest expletive ever to have passed his lips - and this only after extreme provocation. But now, finding himself the unwilling participant in a subterfuge, something inside was urging him to harden his outlook. He realised that he was going to need an extra strength to get himself through the next twenty-four hours, that a choirmaster alone was sadly inadequate to the task facing him. So he turned to George England for help.

Once back inside the tiny terraced house where he lived, he made his preparations for the work that he needed to do. Never had a challenge such as this presented itself to him: why should it have done? But life has a habit of putting unexpected obstacles in the path of all and, to date, the choirmaster had led a relatively trouble free life. Now it was his turn to prove that he could deal with life's trials and tribulations and, in doing so, would avoid certain facial rearrangement. His first move was to stand in front of his bathroom mirror and look at himself straight in the eye.

"You are a man!" he told himself, not very convincingly.

He tried again: he told himself that the only place he could get a copy of the letter from was in the private file, kept in the Church vestry. Come hell or high water, he would get there under the cover of darkness and copy it. His reflection absorbed all of this information calmly, and then gave him a sickly grin. It then reminded him that he was completely unused to undertaking such an errand and, furthermore, that he was a fool if he believed for one moment that he could be successful. Choirmasters, he lectured himself sternly, should stick to what they know best. Being the master of a choir was good enough for his father and it should be good enough for him! But the ever present spectre of Jack Hatchard's fist, which had grown to immense proportions in his mind's eye, hovered in front of his mouth. He walked away from his reflection in search of the only point of reference in his possession which would aid him in the task ahead.

Some months previously, at a Friday evening choir practice, he had confiscated a comic from one of the choirboys. The little scamp had it hidden behind his hymn book and was reading it instead of paying attention to his part in the hymn. Indeed, so absorbed was he in the story that he did not notice the annoyed choirmaster bearing down upon him. With a few sarcastic comments about young lads who wasted everybody else's time through their own ignorance, the comic was snatched from the boy's hand. But later that night, once at home and relaxing in an armchair, the choirmaster had glanced through the pages of this comic: he too soon became absorbed in its contents. They concerned the exploits of one George England who, as far as the avid reader could discern, was an undercover soldier of sorts. Despite being pitted against an entire enemy army, this cool headed good guy had single-handedly, and effortlessly, won the war all by himself (well, not quite by himself. He was accompanied by a freckle-faced young sapper known by his nickname of 'Curly'. But 'Curly' did not do much, apart from continually get himself into scrapes that George England then had to rescue him from. Even the inexperienced choirmaster could see that such an assistant would be a hindrance rather than a help.) It was to this comic that the choirmaster now turned to as a reference book. He knew that within its pages he would learn the techniques of operating under a veil of darkness. And George England, not having any wars to win at that particular time, was more than happy to assist a choirmaster in his hour of need.

So it was that, an hour later, he was ready for his sortie. For the most part the preparation had been far easier than he imagined: it was just a question of ensuring that everything he wore was as dark as possible. As his wardrobe tended toward sombre clothing, as he had always felt befitted a man in his position, it was no difficulty to select the trousers and jacket he would wear. Following George's advice he made sure that these were the most comfortable items that he possessed, essential for ease of movement. The shirt had been a slight problem - he only had white ones to choose from. But George pointed out that a good undercover agent had to think on his feet, he had to learn the art of improvisation. If this meant that a white shirt, stained with the contents of a bottle of ink, had to be sacrificed to the greater cause, then so be it. Unfortunately the ink did not have time to dry on the nylon before the choirmaster had to don the garment, thus causing a small discomfort to the wearer. But this was of little consequence as the intrepid pair stood in front of the bathroom mirror to inspect their progress so far. Satisfied that the clothing was adequate, it now came time to apply a thick layer of shoe polish to face, neck, ears and bald pate of 'The Creeper'.

'The Creeper': the shadowy figure who slipped out of the house just after midnight was no longer the choirmaster. He now had a code name, one that he was rather pleased with. It gave him the air of one who moved stealthily through the night with confidence. He needed confidence. He also desperately needed a means whereby he could rid himself of a nagging feeling of guilt over his actions. Tonight it was not the choirmaster who was breaking the trust of his position within the Church, it was 'The Creeper', special agent, who made his way to the darkness of the churchyard. For this short journey George England had proved himself to be an invaluable guide, always spotting and pointing out the brighter areas of the street to avoid and steering his protege in the direction of the dark spots. Only at one juncture had he doubted his mentor: he had to pass a house where a light was streaming from a downstairs window, the occupants were in the room beyond and the curtains were open. As he hesitated, afraid to pass, George assured him that it would be safe to do so by pointing out that the people within would only see an anonymous form walking by, they would assume him to be one making their way home and think nothing of it. Not entirely convinced of this, 'The Creeper', after many heart thumping minutes pressed against the wall of this house, decided that discretion was the better part of valour and crawled on his hands and knees until he had passed the window.

Once having reached the darkness of the churchyard he paused, hidden in a recess in the wall of this imposing building. Here he took a few minutes to regain his breath and to reinforce in his mind that he was 'The Creeper': special agent. His passage this far had not been strenuous by any means: at least, not in terms of physical energy. But it had greatly taken its toll on his nerves, not only for the reason of his being a novice at this kind of action, but also due to the risk factor. George had explained it carefully during the briefing by breaking the operation into three parts: First; getting from his home to the churchyard. The likelihood of being observed was at its greatest due to having to manoeuvre through a residential area. Second; having attained the first objective, the darkness of the churchyard would reduce the chance of being spotted. However, if he was seen in this place at this time it would appear to be highly suspicious to a passerby. To reduce the risk of a subsequent alarm being raised, it would be prudent to move as swiftly as discretion permitted to the third objective: which was inside the Church itself. Inside this building he was at his safest as it could be assumed to be empty: furthermore, the chances of any other person deciding to visit the Church at night were low. 'The Creeper' was keen to reach the third objective without delay but, before abandoning the cover afforded by the recess, he slowly moved his head forward in order to peer back along the route he had taken. He stared for a full minute into the gloom before his impatience got the better of him: convincing himself that the coast was clear he took a few deep breaths to steady his nerves. Then, promising himself that he would return to being a choirmaster very soon, he moved carefully around the outside of the building to the small side door.

Access to the Church through this door would be the easiest part of the whole operation, as he had explained to George when questioned on this point during the briefing. He was a trusted key holder to the building, although how he would ever be able to think of himself as 'trusted' from this night hence he did not know, the word seemed to stick in his throat as he spoke it. But the new-found undercover agent within him, not entirely convincingly, told him he must deal with this problem only once the present operation was completed. With this in mind, he quietly unlocked and opened the door, crept over the threshold and then closed and locked the door behind himself. He was in and there was now no turning back until he had seen the job through.

So concerned had 'The Creeper' been on the first two stages of the venture, he had given no thought as to what would actually happen once he gained entry to the Church. The reality of being suddenly surrounded by an almost total darkness therefore came as a shock to him. To be fair, George had tried to warn him during the briefing that he would need time to adjust his vision, that to try and move around too soon would only result in collisions with the pews. But, in this instance, pre-warned did not amount to pre-armed: 'The Creeper', finding himself in a place that he would never have wished to have entered alone at night, felt an overwhelming desire to make a noise. He found the silence terrifying, a fear that could only be quashed by his calling out to ask if anyone was there. In his mind a battle of wits ensued, the carefully chosen words of his friend and mentor seeking to gain prominence over the need to hear the sound of his own voice. What comfort this would be to the choirmaster trapped within the body of an undercover agent! Then as his eyes started giving him the benefit of night vision a new terror made its presence known: shadows. Not the usual shadows to be found everywhere, the sort created by a light casting its glow over an object, these were shadows that moved around in the dark with no outside agency to create or control them. As he stared in horror a row of silhouettes assumed the shape of monks kneeling in prayer in a corner of the nave, their cowled heads clearly visible against the wall beyond. A woman stood in a corner, unmoving and barely distinguishable but staring unwaveringly at him. To her right, and towering over her, stood a giant: no ordinary giant this, it was the one who he remembered from his childhood, the one who appeared in a television commercial to increase the sale of tinned sweetcorn. Logic told him that these things could not possibly be there in reality, his brain ordered him to run forward and chase these spectres away, they had no right to be there. Noise would destroy them, noise would.....

"Stop your knees knocking together!" the voice of George England hissed suddenly in his left ear, "The racket is enough to bring every Vicar in a fifty mile radius down upon us!"

The words had the effect of instantly calming him and the figures so lately intimidating him melted into nothing as he looked at them anew. He was not alone, he had George beside him: he could come to no harm, certainly not from shadows that belonged in 1960s television advertisements. With this comfort came also renewed determination to complete his task with the minimum of delay. Once this was done he would be able to return to the safety of his home: he started to make his way toward the Vestry.

"Shoes!" whispered George, the lowness of his voice doing little to remove its tone of urgency, "Take your shoes off. Now!"

But this order was not really necessary: realising how loud his footsteps sounded in the large empty building, 'The Creeper' was already bending to remove his footwear.

Putting his shoes to one side of the door for retrieval on his way out, he proceeded on stockinged feet to the Vestry.

For weeks afterwards the memory of those few short yards would haunt his dreams - as well as giving the occasional cold sweat to his waking hours. He could feel many eyes upon him: The saints, the dead, the angels themselves. Blinkered, 'The Creeper' ignored them all. But not without great discomfort, he could feel their disapproval every inch of the way.

"It's all very well for them," muttered George England cynically, "Sat up there on their exalted thrones. Anybody would think they didn't know that there's a war going on down here!"

'The Creeper' took great heart from these words as he soundlessly opened the door to the Vestry, he knew that George understood his reasons for acting so out of character: this amounted to approval for what others may view as highly disgraceful behaviour. Small comfort, but reassuring nevertheless. Having gained access to this inner sanctum no time was wasted in opening the filing cabinet and locating the letter which he needed to copy. These two sheets of foolscap contained very little of substance and, for the first time since his untimely encounter with Jack Hatchard, he found himself wondering why the information was being sought. Glancing at the pages he saw merely an outline of the man's career, a few biographical details, his academic record and his stated hopes for the future of the parish which was to be his new post.

"You can read it later if you want to, for now just copy it. Don't forget we are behind enemy lines here. The sooner we're in de-brief, the better."

Brought back to the moment by the words of George England, 'The Creeper' acted upon them with no further delay. Crawling under a large table, from where the light of a candle would be less visible through the high windows, he made a faithful copy of the details. As he did so, raised to anger by the sight of the Vicar's name in cold print, 'The Creeper' started regaining his persona as the choirmaster. But not the meek and mild version of his old self that would be recognised by his neighbours, this was a man who realised that The Reverend Michael Grape was the cause of his present situation. He knew not why the Vicar had become the focus of attention to such unsavoury men as Jack Hatchard but, recalling the frightening interview he himself had undergone in this very room, he was now in the mind that the man deserved it. The adrenaline coursing through his system gave the choirmaster the clarity to complete his task methodically, he no longer needed a code name nor an excuse for his actions. He now had a justification for being caught up in this subterfuge, he was an avenging choirmaster striking a blow for put-upon choirmasters everywhere. It was a very different man who crawled out from under the table fifteen minutes later: his copying complete, he replaced the letter in its file. He then turned to George England and spoke with a controlled menace.

"Got it. Now the Vicar will get his just rewards!"

"Good work," whispered George, "Now let's get out of here and back to base. But carefully. Let's not spoil it now we've got this far."

This was advice that the choirmaster was so keen to follow that, despite his best efforts to ensure that he left no trace of his presence in the Church, he did make one mistake: it was not until he closed his own front door behind himself that he realised a grave oversight. He had left his shoes in the Church. How, he asked himself, could he have not noticed the lack of footwear on his way back from the sortie: he knew the answer to this even as the question formed in his mind. His anger at the Vicar and his determination to get home without delay had combined to make him numb to anything else. He turned to his friend and mentor for advice but unfortunately, immediately upon entering the house, George had climbed back into the pages of the comic never to return to the world of non-heroes. As was his wont, once his mission was complete, the ultra modest George England simply melted into the background leaving his enemies baffled and his rescued grateful. Nor could the choirmaster summon up enough of his avenger role to face retracing his steps back to the Church to retrieve them: the put-upon choirmasters of the world would now have to fend for themselves. For himself he just wanted the night to be over, he wanted it to be a year hence and this whole episode consigned to history. Wearily he climbed the stairs to his small bathroom: here he spent the rest of the night in only partially successful attempts to remove the shoe polish from his person. During the course of this clean - up operation his tired mind worked hard to convince him that his shoes could not possibly be traced back to their owner.

Chapter Twelve

The Reverend Michael Grape had cause to feel great joy and to be more than a little pleased with himself. He was feeling inspired and the source of his inspiration stemmed from a very touching letter which had been hand-posted through his door during the previous night.

Dear vicer, it read,
I aint been to church befor becos I aint nown to and now I no thats rong. I want to go to church now and I no I got to learn cermanments but thats ok. Now I no I best goin to church I will be good at it and you aint goin to be sory to se me ther. Fid says to rite to you cos then you nos to look owt for me and help me be good at church things. Fid says to tell you im a fisherman cos churchs tret them speshal cos sumone in the bibel were a fisherman to. I rekon you must ave red that bit aniway. I got to go way for a cuple of days an will se you wen I gets bac. I not norty not like sum I no I jus aint lernt bout church yet boatook bald

The Vicar was not to know that this letter had been devised purely as a means whereby Boathook Bald could gather information: 'The Dirt' as Fiddler Crabbe had called it, thereby paraphrasing the Admiral's solicitor friend. The conspirators had seen this as a good way for the prawnman to become part of the congregation quickly, he could then catch the Vicar and Miss Simpson red-handed. From then on it would be a simple act of blackmail: easy! Easy, that is, under the influence of the large amount of cider which had been the fuel for the plan. Once the pair had agreed on this project they wasted no time in putting it into action: they worked together to compose a letter to the Vicar on a piece of paper which Leggy had kindly given them. It was not the cleanest of pieces of paper but, under the flickering candlelight in Paradise, this fact had not been apparent to the conspirators. With a lack of any writing implement to hand, Fiddler Crabbe had collected together a goodly pile of spent matchsticks from the nearby ashtrays: with their blackened tips wetted by dipping them into the small pool of saliva which they had created on the table, each one was good for three or four words. It had been a laborious task, interspersed with much disagreement on the subject of spelling. But once the missive was completed the friends congratulated themselves. They felt sure that The Reverend Michael Grape would respond favourably to these words which, upon receiving them, he most certainly did: but not quite in the manner in which the authors had hoped for.

Despite the rather grubby, dog-eared and cider stained condition of the paper, its message was viewed by the Vicar as Divine Intervention: a lost soul wished to seek the Word. And, in doing so at this particular moment in time, he had provided the answer to a question very much on the Vicar's mind. Namely, what to do with The Ship's Captains Reading Rooms once the prawnmen had vacated it. For it was The Reverend Michael Grapes fervent wish that the use of this building should be changed irrevocably, that never again would it house the prawnmen. He needed to think of an alternative use for The Club and then he could take over the lease for the Church: but he was aware that in order to raise the necessary funds from within his parish he would have to present a reason to prevail upon their generosity. And so he had prayed and, with the arrival of this letter, he knew that his prayers had been answered.

The Vicar realised that he had two considerations to take into account with regards to this particular lost soul. That the fisherman had turned to him in order to gain salvation was a call not to be ignored: indeed, it was seen by the Vicar as a credit to his mission that such people felt that they could turn to him in their moment of need knowing that they would be welcomed by the Church. But, by the Church did not necessarily mean into the Church, that is, into the building itself. The Reverend Michael Grape did not wish to stand in the pulpit and see, or smell, this so obviously scruffy individual sat on one of his pews. Nor did he consider it right and proper to subject his congregation to one who, without doubt, would be as stained and as dog-eared as his letter was. And this is where the Ship's Captains Reading Rooms could be utilised, for if there was one lost soul among the fishermen then surely there must be more. These men, the Vicar reasoned, needed a place of their own, close to their work, where they could go when they wished to pray. And so was born the scheme for the 'Fishermens' Praying Rooms', perfectly situated upon the Town Quay. Once he had formed this idea in his mind he was then able to envisage it: the men stepping ashore from their craft and heading straight to prayer, grateful to have this facility provided by the Church. 'For those in peril on the sea' would be the name for a fundraising campaign in the parish and The Vicar determined to start planning this without delay.

~~*~~

The Visitor looked out of the window of his lodgings at a May morning which, after a promising start, had turned dull and grey. The outlook was not good, there was a definite threat of rain darkening the cloud base, but this could not dampen his optimism. He dropped his gaze downwards to the writing pad on the table before him: these pages contained his notes, looking at them he decided that his bosses back at the office would be satisfied. He had sufficient information on the prawnmen to give a comprehensive view of their way of life and, as if to place a seal upon this resolve, he gathered up all of the pages and slid them carefully into a cardboard folder. Quite what they would be able to do with this latest offering, the Visitor thought to himself, was anybody's guess. As he had read through his interim report he could not help thinking that most of it was just too bizarre, those who had not experienced the sincerity behind the prawnman's telling of it would find it hard to credit. Someone should write a book about it, he told himself: though, on reflection, he knew that if this was to happen, why, nobody would ever believe that it was true! Putting all of these thoughts to one side, along with the cardboard folder, he made himself ready for his daily stroll to the Town Cellars. When he met with Boathook Bald that day he would have a short formal chat and let the man know his services were no longer required. Then, the Visitor told himself happily, despite the downturn in the weather he would enjoy the rest of his stay in the town as a holiday.

In a moment of abandon he broke from a tiny part of his daily routine: no, he told himself firmly, today I will not wear a tie. The immediate sense of illicit freedom this gave him was, he found, exciting. If only his colleagues could see him, walking out of the house half dressed, they would be rendered speechless through shock. The Visitor moved in circles where the size, shape and colour of ones neck-tie was a highly competitive issue: it separated the men from the boys, the wheat from the chaff and the aspirants from the elite. In the eyes of his peers to be seen in public without this item of clothing was unthinkable but the Visitor cared not. It has to be pointed out that this act of defiance was bolstered up by the sure knowledge that he would not be seen by any who knew him. Once he was ready to leave the house, and still elated by his temporary sartorial code, he ran lightly down the stairs and out of the front door. His gait was carefree, reflecting the pleasure that he felt at now being on holiday for a few days: bliss! But then the Visitor was not to know that his future was being decided by some who knew not the subtle niceties of neck wear. From the window of a cafe opposite his lodgings three pairs of eyes were watching him with great interest.

"That's our man." Derek Lipton, the owner of one of the pairs of eyes told his brothers, the owners of the other two pairs. "We will have to play this one carefully, taking an officer aint so easy. But I've got an idea....."

~~*~~

"I got t'go 'way f'r a couple o'days."

Boathook Bald's greeting to the Visitor was apologetic and tinged with more than a little regret. Due to his dealings with the Visitor since their first meeting he had given his imagination free rein: he fondly pictured day after day spent drinking at his benefactor's expense, so much so that he had been delving deep into his memory desperate to dredge up anything which could be construed as a custom or a tradition.

"The '*Joan* is on 'er way in." he added by way of explanation.

"The *'Joan'*?" enquired the Visitor who, as we have seen, was not in the least bit disappointed to hear this news, "Is there a problem with this?"

"Could be." stated the prawnman. He then proceeded to give the Visitor an account of how the boarders supplied such ships with a crew. The recipient of this information listened with growing amazement: if he had not, since arriving in this town, heard and seen so much which beggared belief he would not have credited it with an ounce of accuracy. As it was he reprimanded himself for breaking a golden rule: never go anywhere without a notepad and pencil. You never know what is around the next corner.

"O'course," Boathook Bald was saying, "The boarders don't us'ally touch none o'us local boys, they goes f'r the visitin' deep sea 'ands. But if they gets desp'rate..."

He left the sentence unfinished, the implied danger hanging in the air between them. In the slight pause that followed the Visitor felt an inexplicable shudder travel up his spine. This was accompanied by a momentary sense of personal danger to himself but, not being used to such psychic warnings, he shrugged it off and put it out of his mind as he asked;

"So where will you go?"

"Ah, well, there's a little islan' up the top o'the bay" the prawnman pointed vaguely in the direction of the harbour. "We all gets up there f'r a couple o'days. The boarders knows where we are but they also knows they won't get us easy, we c'n see 'em comin' a mile off an' get 'idden. An' at low water the bay 'roun' the islan' dries out an' it's all mud up there y'see. They couldn't get to us if they tried. So we only needs t'keep a look out when the tide's in, the rest o'the time we c'n relax."

There was heard a distant rumble of thunder and, simultaneously, the two men looked skywards. The clouds overhead gave no indication of rain but there was a sudden stillness in the air, the subtle thickening of the atmosphere which preceded a thunderstorm.

"I'd best be off t'beat this bit o'weather," said Boathook Bald. "The *'Joan'* is due in t'morrow. Cap'n Coates leaves the crewin' t'the boarders while 'e goes off in search o'Arse Islan' an' then in two day's time 'e'll be off again. That's when we comes back t'town y'see an' so I'll be seein' you then."

"Did you say 'Arse Island'? Where is..."

The prawnman interrupted the question with a great roar of laughter. "Arse Islan'? It's wherever 'e c'n find it!" he answered. "It's what a sailor says y'see. If y'was out in a boat an' the wind gets up then y'goes an' finds a bit o'land that'll give y'shelter from it. Say y'was out in the channel near the Isle o' Wight an' a blow comes up from the west. Well, y'd go roun' the east o'the Isle where it's calmer. So then y'd be under the lee o'the Isle o' Wight y'see."

"Yes, I see, but..." the Visitor got no further before he was interrupted once more.

"So when a sailor gets ashore an' 'e goes off t'find a bed an' a bit o'comp'ny t'share it, well, then 'e says 'e's spendin' the night under the lee o'Arse Islan'!"

Leaving the somewhat naïve Visitor to make of this what he could, Boathook Bald waved a hand in farewell before setting off to hide from the boarders. During his explanation regarding their mode of business, he had not mentioned the Lipton Boys by name: to commit such an indiscretion would be unthinkable. But this wisdom in protecting the boarders' family name, and therefore himself, left the Visitor unaware that his subsequent dealings with the Liptons should be approached with great caution. But, blissfully ignorant of a plot which he was soon to be drawn into was now in its initial stages, he began to plan his day.

As the Visitor pondered upon which direction his visiting would start, the museum or the pottery showrooms, Derek Lipton was tapping upon the door of Mrs Cousin's lodging house. Without waiting for a reply he opened the door and entered: an action that was accompanied by an instinctive, and in this instance unnecessary, glance each way along the street. This act of ensuring that he was not being observed was superfluous, he did not need an invitation to enter this house: nor would a neighbour who saw him step over this threshold think that anything was amiss. It was the home of his aunt, an aunt who had always treated him as a particularly favoured nephew. Thus, once the door was closed behind him, Derek walked through the hallway toward the kitchen as if he was in his own home. He knew that Mrs Cousins would be sat at the table, it was part of her daily routine: mindful that her guests may be averse to the smell of tobacco smoke she always waited until the house was empty before she allowed herself this, her one and only vice. It was the moment before the indulgence that Derek walked in upon and delayed momentarily with a cheery greeting;

"Hello Gorgeous."

For which he received a fondly admonishing response;

"Get on with you!"

Mrs Cousins had reached an age where such compliments, delivered with the sincerity of a potential suitor, were but a distant memory. She did, however, take great pleasure in the fact that her nephew had used the word as a term of affection: despite the rebuke in her tone she enjoyed his teasing banter. After raising her right cheek to receive his customary kiss, and in the manner of families, she then carried on with what she had been doing before Derek had walked in upon her morning. He, in his turn, proceeded to ignore her and walked across to a cabinet to get himself a cup. Picking out the one that he always used when in this kitchen, he then moved toward the teapot ever kept fresh under the cosy. His aunt, meanwhile, took a match from the box in front of her on the table and, striking it into flame, used it to light her pipe.

The simple act of getting a briar bowlful of tobacco burning satisfactorily is inclined to create a lot of smoke: it was through such a haze that Derek, having poured himself a cup of tea, next addressed his aunt.

"Good news," he said as he seated himself opposite her at the table, "We can get that decorating done for you this week."

"Decorating? What decorating?" the old lady was confused and this showed in both her tone and expression.

"Don't you remember? You were saying last month that the guest room needed a lick of paint before the summer season."

Mrs Cousins looked blankly at the amiable nephew who knew full well that she would have no recollection of this whatsoever: she had not asked for any painting to be done. He also knew that the room in question was not in need of redecoration, it had been done only eighteen months beforehand and would require no further attention for a few years hence. But Derek also knew that his aunt would not be able to resist having her nephews around for a few days, it would give her the opportunity to fuss over them. Having borne no children of her own, she would not turn away from a chance to mother her surrogate sons and this suited his purpose perfectly.

"Well Derek, it's a good job I've got you boys to remember these things for me." she said at length, "You know what I'm like for always forgetting things."

"Don't worry about that," replied Derek, wearing his best cheeky-little-boy grin, "It's your age!"

"Oh no, it's not that! I've been forgetful for as long as I can remember." Mrs Cousins, after making this observation, puffed on her pipe in the contented manner of one who has learned to live with their shortcomings.

"So," continued Derek, "We'll be round to look at it tomorrow. I think we've got a few days clear."

"That's very kind of you Derek, I'm sure. And I will have time to bake some cakes for you to have with... Oh dear, no, you can't do it this week!" Mrs Cousins suddenly remembered that she had a guest staying, "I've got a young man in there at the moment. He was supposed to be gone by now but he booked another week. Paid in advance too."

"Oh, that is a nuisance." the crafty boarder feigned thoughtfulness, "I don't know when we will get the chance otherwise, you know how busy we get. It's a pity, I could almost taste those delicious cakes of yours."

"Well, if it's a problem, we can always leave it until the end of the summer season." his aunt spoke these words making them sound like this was not an option entirely to her liking. Being now convinced that she had indeed requested this task, the paintwork in the guest room suddenly occupied a place of great urgency in her mind.

"Let me think, I know we've got the Heath contract coming up but supposing we delayed that 'til... oh no, we can't." Derek furrowed his brow as if juggling a full calender around in his mind, "I suppose we could fit it in as soon as your guest leaves, maybe... Although, no, old man Brown needs us next week. Don't worry Aunty, There has to be an answer."

After another few moments seemingly deep in thought, Derek suddenly clicked his fingers in the air and adopted the expression of one who has just realised that the answer to a problem was not only simple, it was also so obvious as to be a great bafflement that he had not seen it straight away.

"I've got it!" he announced, "We have rooms spare at our place at the moment. Why not explain the situation to your young man and ask him if he would mind moving in with us? We'll give him something overlooking the Town Quay, I'm sure he'd like that."

"But he's paid me..." began Mrs Cousins.

"That's ok, you tuck that money into your purse. We're not going to be worried about a week's rent, it's not as if we'd have anyone in there at this time of the year anyway so we're not exactly losing out. The main thing is to get your decorating done Aunty."

"You boys are so kind to me." Mrs Cousins felt tears brimming in her doting eyes, so completely did she fail to see the rogue sat in her kitchen, "I will mention it to him when he comes in this afternoon."

And, two hours later upon the return of the Visitor, mention it she did. At first her guest seemed dubious, he was finding life with Mrs Cousins much to his liking. But two factors eventually swayed his decision to agree to the suggestion: firstly, and clearly, was the tempting offer of the room overlooking the Town Quay. This, he felt, would be the crowning glory of his stay in this place, the ship's Captain looking out upon the bustle of the port. The second factor was due to a more subtle influence: when introduced to the Lipton Boys they were at their persuasive best. To all intents and purposes the Visitor's new landlords could not do enough to make him welcome. But to ensure his co-operation in their plan the brothers did manage to evoke a subliminal inference: that, were he to refuse, not only would he be causing an inconvenience to Mrs Cousins but also, by implication, he would be saying that there was something wrong with his new lodgings.

Faced with these undeniable facts, the Visitor agreed to the move whereupon the wolves in sheeps' clothing exchanged secret triumphant smiles: one way or another the Lipton Boys always got their wish.

Chapter Thirteen

Jack Hatchard paid a visit to the choirmaster at the appointed time to receive the copy of the letter. In view of his previous dealings with Jack this was a meeting which the choirmaster had anticipated with no great relish: but he need not have worried. Although he enjoyed his reputation as a bruiser Jack Hatchard liked to think that he was a fair man, 'firm but fair' was just one of his mottoes. As he had, at their first encounter, assured the choirmaster that his co-operation would result in no physical violence against his person then, as he knocked upon the man's front door, the very idea of displaying a threatening manner was far from his mind. This eventuality would only come about if, and only if, his request had not been fulfilled. Therefore, upon opening his front door, the choirmaster found himself being treated as a well respected business associate. Taken by surprise he simply and wordlessly handed over an envelope which contained that which he had been ordered to supply. Privately he was hoping that this would be the end of his dealings with Jack Hatchard, but the delighted recipient of the envelope did not intend to leave without expressing his gratitude. He was pleased to have done business with the man and made a great point of telling him so: it was, he stated, truly a pleasure and he looked forward to meeting him again. Furthermore, if his new found co-conspirator ever needed Jack to smack someone in the mouth then he only had to ask and, he was assured, it would be done without charge. This offer was made as a reward for the help that the choirmaster had given Jack: 'always return a favour with a favour', that was just another of Jack Hatchard's mottoes. In reply, the benefactor of this kind offer made it known that this service was not required at that precise moment, but he would certainly bear this generous offer in mind and that Jack was too kind. During the course of this, seemingly grateful, speech the choirmaster once again found his knees to be knocking together forcibly. The effect of this involuntary movement was causing his voice to adopt a somewhat higher pitch than was usual but, as all previous discourse between the two men had taken place with the ones throat held tightly by the other, Jack Hatchard assumed this to be the choirmaster's normal mode of speech. It would not have entered the bruiser's mind that it was due to his new-found friend's fervent wish for Jack Hatchard to be elsewhere. In this, it transpired, he did not have long to wait as the letter needed to be delivered without delay. Jack only tarried further in order to extend an open invitation for the choirmaster to join him for a drink in the 'Mucky Duck' one evening. Then, with a cheerful farewell, he set off to the home of Master Miles: here the letter could be exchanged for payment in lieu of Jack's specialist services.

It was an impatient Admiral who finally came to open this envelope, the hours since he had first contacted Jack having passed too slowly for one with so little time to solve a major problem. This impatience, however, was not to be immediately curbed by a glance at its contents, so audaciously copied at no little risk by 'The Creeper'. Master Miles had known that it was an uncertainty as to whether the information obtained would be of any use, but the reality of seeing such scant details on paper made his heart sink. Schooling details filled four lines, further education another four. Then followed some three lines about a career in the armed services before the next page and a half told of his various good works in the service of the Church. This, thought the Admiral bitterly, has been a waste of time, money and effort, there was nothing on these pages that could even slightly incriminate the Vicar. He went to bed that night with a much more troubled mind, fully aware that he had placed far too much hope upon the letter: in the morning he would have to think afresh.

But when the morning came, while Boathook Bald lay upon the Island making his own plans for dealing with the Vicar, Master Miles found himself unable to put the letter to one side and forget about it. Nor, he soon realised, was he to gain anything by his continually taking it from its envelope to reread it: but he was starting to feel that his initial disappointment regarding this scant information had been an overreaction, that he had been too hasty to dismiss its possible worth. On the other hand, as he acknowledged, an answer did not spring forth easily from the pages, much to the Admiral's frustration. Finally he put the letter into his shirt pocket and fastened the button over it: he decided that he would concentrate on just one thing at a time, starting with his breakfast. Later that morning he would go to The Club where he would study the letter more carefully and until then it would stay in his pocket. Not only would The Club give him quieter surroundings than his home (where the housekeepers seemed that day to be unable to perform the simplest of jobs without creating excessive noise) but being in situ would focus his mind more clearly.

This decided, he tackled a plateful of food which, he quickly found, had become less than appetising due to its heat being lost whilst he had been paying too much heed to the letter. With each mouthful subsequently being something of a minor ordeal to chew upon he then realised that there was another distraction that morning which he had barely been aware of: the occasional high pitched chatter of children passing through the lane outside of the dining room window. They were making their way excitedly and noisily toward the quay and Master Miles, despite himself, could not help but wonder why. There must be something special happening today: this thought flitted through his mind as he abandoned the cold breakfast and prepared himself to leave the house. Somewhere, in a corner of his memory, he was sure that he should know what this something was but, with all of his attention addressed to the problem in hand, he could not recall any details. No matter: he had one or two errands to attend to in the High Street, mundane tasks which he would welcome for their normality. Then he would go to The Club to read the letter with new eyes. As he was the type of person who sometimes needed to expend energy in order to assist with his thinking he wasted no more time in wondering about the youngsters. Once ready he hurriedly left the house.

But as the Admiral of the Prawning Fleet made his way through the town he could not focus his thoughts upon his errands. Instead they still dwelt upon the letter concerning The Reverend Michael Grape: an instinct was now telling him that within these pages was the answer to the prawnmens' dilemma. Gone was the doubt of the night before, replaced by a growing sense that he had missed something of significance in those bare details on the Vicar. But what was it? Where was it?

"The trouble is," he murmured, "I can't see the sea for the spray. I need something to clear my head."

As if Neptune himself had stepped in to lend a helping hand, no sooner had he voiced this thought than his wish was granted. Noticing that yet another group of youngsters were making their eager way to the quay he suddenly realised what day it was: the *'Joan'* was heading into port! How on earth could he have forgotten this? Putting aside his errands, which now paled into insignificance, he turned on his heel and quickly made his way to The Club. Hoping against hope that he was not too late he made his way up the stairs to the main room two at a time. Inside this inner sanctum he noted that several other Masters were already there, grouped around the open widows. Smiling broadly, and showing as much excitement as that displayed by the youngsters, they turned to greet him as he entered.

"Master Miles!" said one of their number, "We thought you were going to miss it."

"Not for the world!" replied their Admiral spiritedly, "Today of all days I need a bit of sport!"

The 'bit of sport' to which he referred to concerned the unfortunate sailors who were now approaching the Town Quay on board the *'Joan'*. As always, these men would display no hesitation in making their escape from the ship as soon as the last rope was made fast around its bollard. And by way of adding injury to insult, the local schoolchildren were there to pelt them with missiles as they did so: it had become a local tradition associated with the arrival of the *'Joan'*. It was an event which brought many of the townsfolk hither to enjoy the spectacle and to add voices of encouragement to the childrens' efforts. Eggs, flour, stones, anything that the youngsters could lay their hands on would be utilised as the terrified sailors ran the gauntlet of the attack. They were safe in the knowledge that these poor men were sensible only to the need to get away from Captain Coates and this meant that there was no fear of them retaliating: to stand and fight against this onslaught could mean possible recapture. As an added bonus to the day's entertainment, upon the promise of a generous shower of sweets, the attackers would ensure that the sailors had to run past the windows of The Club. From this vantage point the Prawning Masters, catapults at the ready, would fire empty winkle shells at the fleeing men.

A loud cheering breaking out suddenly amongst the townsfolk was a clear signal that the sailors were on their way. Being well practised in this event, the crowd would form themselves in such a way as to ensure that the victims could go in one direction only: toward their assailants. These latter awaited their targets eagerly yet they loosed their missiles at their own leisure, maximum damage for minimum effort was the rule. To this end the sailors' passage would be hampered for a while by the mass of spectators moving in to surround them. Trapped within an inescapable circle, they were kept at the mercy of their tormentors until all ammunition was spent.

Once they were allowed to escape this initial onslaught the men would then face a far more calculated attack from the Prawning Masters. This part of the mornings' proceedings was born of the Masters' great need to wager against each other at every possible opportunity, with Sweaty Betty holding the unenviable post of scorekeeper. She would award points using a system even more confusing than that used at a cricket match: factors taken into account included the number of shells loosed by each individual, the number of hits, how many different targets were hit, where they were hit, total blood loss incurred and the average of the same per shell expended. It was due to the high points awarded for blood loss which accounted for the fact that winkle shells were used: rarely did they fail to break skin.

The Prawning Masters saw nothing malicious in this game,

it was purely and simply another chance for their wagering. Nor did any of the townsfolk witnessing the event ever speak out against the welcome that these visiting sailors received in their town. The victims were common seafarers down on their luck, the lowest of the low. Though governments throughout the world, and throughout the centuries, would gratefully accept their willing service in times of a national crisis, outside of these times they were viewed as being a pest by all. And if governments, by Royal Assent, could misuse its seamen, then why not the commoners. And besides, the town had its own share of poor sailors and no room was seen for more. Furthermore, if their rapid departure from the town could provide a little entertainment for its citizens, then so much the better: it would make them think twice about returning to these shores. Rather that than having them hanging around the wharves and making a nuisance of themselves. With these, and other equally superficial arguments, the town justified its disgraceful treatment of these poor wretches.

When the last shanghiied seafarer had escaped his tormentors, Master Miles retired to his armchair with a glass of whiskey. Usually a fierce competitor when taking part in anything which involved wagering against his fellow Masters, today saw him more so: in his mind he had not seen the unfortunates as sailors, he had imagined each and every one of them as the Vicar. It was a crude form of self delusion, this he knew, but it had worked: it was with greater clarity of mind that he now approached the letter. Once settled into the armchair he took it from his pocket and unfolded it upon his lap. All around him was the chatter of his fellow Masters disagreeing with each other about the merits, or otherwise, of differing makes of catapult. The Admiral knew that their excitement, generated by the wagering, would soon pass and the room would quieten. When, eventually, this peace came, Master Miles looked down at the letter and immediately one word leapt out of the page for his attention: Liverpool. Upon closer inspection this word proved to be part of a paragraph giving details of The Mission to Seamen in that northern port. The Reverend Michael Grape, during the early part of his calling to the cloth, had spent some time based at this mission. There were no further details beyond the basic facts but reading this short paragraph caused the Admiral to suppress an excited smile of relief. His sixth sense now told him that Liverpool held the key to solving their dilemma, but this would depend upon the outcome of a phone call that he would need to make. He turned to one of his colleagues and spoke without betraying any of the optimism which was gradually growing within.

"Geoff, what is the name of that scouser who comes down sometimes? The one we always get in for a glass or two."

"Which one? There were two who used to come down, but one of them died. He was called Terry as far as I remember. The other one was called..."

Here Master Geoff Rose of the Prawning Vessel *'Kate'* adopted his thoughtful pose. This posture involved him staring at the ceiling and protruding his lower lip.

"...Harry," he said eventually, turning his gaze toward the bookshelf in a corner of the room, "Harry Winston. We've got his number in the contacts book, if he's still at the same place. We've not seen or heard from him for a few years."

He walked over to the bookcase and removed a thin volume from its shelves.

Handing the book to Master Miles he remarked, in his usual morose fashion.

"He's probably dead too for all we know."

Choosing to ignore this eventuality, the Admiral took the book and searched through its pages to find Harry Winston's phone number. Once this was located and copied into his notebook he rose from his seat, as he did so he noticed that all eyes in the room were now turned expectantly in his direction. Not wishing to raise his own hopes too high, let alone those of his colleagues, he adopted a neutral tone.

"If anyone can come up with some dirt on our friend in the Vicarage, it's our old mate Harry Winston. I can't guarantee it, but knowing the stories that he came out with about life up there he doesn't miss a thing about anyone. It's worth a try."

With these words, and after replacing the contacts book upon the shelf, Master Miles went through to the corner of the kitchen where a telephone sat in a corner of the worktop: this small area was jokingly referred to as 'The Office'. Five minutes later, five long minutes during which Master Rose had tried to eavesdrop to no avail, the Admiral walked back into the room with a wicked, bordering upon evil, gleam in his eye. It was showing more than he would have wished to his fellow Masters but he was unable to suppress his high humour.

"Dirt?" enquired Geoff Rose, voicing the question on all of the assembled Master's lips.

"Better than that," replied their Admiral, "Much, much better than that. I now know how to deal with The Reverend Michael Grape."

"I don't suppose you'd care to share this information?"

Which was a superfluous question as Geoff Rose knew exactly what the answer would be.

"I think not. The less people who know about this little caper the better. But," and here Master Miles tapped the side of his nose meaningfully, "If anyone is running a book on us keeping this place, you'd all do well to put a few quid on us still being here next week."

And with that piece of cryptic advice ringing infuriatingly in their ears, the assembled Masters could only wonder as the Admiral of the Prawning Fleet strode out on some private business of his own. Within moments of his departure speculation amongst them was rife, speculation which took only a very short time to descend into some determined wagering over what the Admiral had discovered. Though they all knew that this was a pointless exercise, each was convinced that they had the answer and were willing to put money upon it. But of one thing they were all certain: that their Club was now saved. Something in the Admiral's manner when he returned from the office had left them in no doubt of this.

Chapter Fourteen

One week later...
The sudden disappearance of The Reverend Michael Grape from within their midst caused no little stir amongst his parishioners, especially as he had fled during the night without prior warning. Indeed, he appeared to be in so much haste to depart the town that he left with very little save the clothes that he stood up in. Then all was explained, but only by way of the rumours: he had done this sort of thing before, many years ago in his youth. The teenage girl whose belly he had filled with an untimely blessing, now a grown woman, had finally tracked him down and travelled hither from Liverpool. Belief in this rumour was fuelled by the fact that a woman who would fit the description, with an accent from outside of the county, was seen by many of the townsfolk on the very day that the Vicar disappeared. More than this: she was accompanied by a young man who could well have been her son and whose features strongly resembled those of the Vicar's. Obviously the son had grown curious about his father and had wished to meet him: the townsfolk saw this as a perfectly valid reason for their journey to the town. Needless to say, most of those who remembered seeing this woman only did so after hearing the rumour.

But no, said another version of the same rumour, it was the girl's father who had been looking for him and, after a search lasting for many years, he had eventually tracked him down. Though The Reverend Michael Grape had long forgotten the girl, and was completely unaware that she had borne him a son, the father had a longer memory. Never a man to whom forgiveness came naturally, he had been pleased to receive an anonymous phone call alerting him to the whereabouts of the wayward Romeo. He had contacted The Reverend Michael Grape and informed him that he was on his way to the town to create a scandal: he had been outraged to discover that the cause of his daughter's ruin now wore a dog-collar. And, dog-collar or not, a bit of old-fashioned justice was to be meted out to a scoundrel! Her father? Nonsense said those in the know. It was her husband, whom the young Mr Grape had cuckolded. Having only just learned of his betrayal......

Whichever version of events an individual chose to believe did not change one fact and on this all were agreed. The Vicar had portrayed himself as being so good that, obviously, he must have had something to hide. His severity of manner became interpreted as a lack of humanity stemming from a need to cover his own shame. Added to this was a sure belief that the Church authorities had been fully aware of these earlier misdeeds, that is why they had dispatched the Vicar to a mission far away from the scene of his indiscretions, to this very town, where he could be kept out of the spotlight. Such was the power of the rumour mill, ever to be trusted even more than photographic evidence, that by the time the Church authorities discovered his disappearance and contacted the police, gossip had become fact. There was nobody questioned in the town found to be unconvinced that the man had run away from his past.

The Admiral of the Prawning Fleet did not listen to such tittle-tattle: not for him the gossip of the common folk, it would hardly become one such as he to indulge himself in town scandal. Having said that, of these particular rumours he was quite proud: but this was only because he had invented them and was pleased with their success. Standing by his drinks cabinet at The Club he poured two glasses of wine. One of these he handed to Sweaty Betty, to whom he had entrusted the task of spreading his fabrications around the town. This most dependable of allies, though harbouring no bitterness over her public pillorying in the past, nevertheless derived a gentle satisfaction from this assignment: she enjoyed the humour of a trick played against one who had wronged her family with his harsh sermonising.

"Good work Betty," he raised his glass to her in a toast, "and thank you. We have signed our part of the lease, it is now just waiting upon the Church to decide who will ratify it instead of Captain Grape. A mere formality."

Apart from Master Miles and the faithful Sweaty Betty only three other people in the town had learnt that the Vicar, before being called into the service of God, had served in the Royal Navy. Whilst the rank of 'Captain' bestowed upon him by Master Miles was an exaggeration he was certainly of sufficient rank to be of interest to the Lipton Boys. It was the three brothers to whom the Admiral had approached upon being informed of the Vicar's seafaring past by Harry Winston, for it was not unknown for the boarders, in return for a fee, to choose a victim that someone wished to see removed from the town. More normally this would tend to be a young man who wanted to be rid of a rival in love or due to a father being over-protective toward a daughter. In this instance the fee was waived as the Lipton Boys were still needing to find an officer for the *'Joan'*. The information passed onto them by Master Miles had come at a timely moment for the brothers: almost as soon as the Visitor had become their guest his unsuitability for the *'Joan'* had become apparent, "The idiot wouldn't even make Cabin

Boy!" Derek had declared, an echo of the Visitor's father's judgement: thus proving that, despite having immersed himself totally in study of maritime matters, sailors are born, not made.

Learning of The Reverend Michael Grape's nautical past had greatly excited the Lipton Boys. The idea of shanghiing a Vicar was one which appealed to them: it was not only a jest which would raise their standing amongst others of their trade throughout the world, it was also a once in a lifetime opportunity. They could not allow the chance to pass them by. So it was that as Master Miles and Sweaty Betty drank wine together, The Reverend Michael Grape was in the Bay of Biscay. As Mate on board the vessel *'Joan'* he had found his world turned upside down in every sense.

"And thank you Harry Winston," the Admiral raised his glass to the useful friend many miles away, "I knew that you wouldn't let me down."

~~*~~

The Vicar, having received a late night call to attend a sick parishioner, was never to know that the message had been sent by the very hale and hearty Lipton Boys. Drinking to their success once the work was done the three brothers were in agreement that it had been a textbook shanghiing: a darkened side-street, an unknowing victim, the deft use of a cosh and a sweetly sleeping body delivered on board the *'Joan'*. It had taken more than a little persuasion to convince Captain Coates that the dog-collared figure who lay before him possessed the necessary skills required to act as first mate aboard his ship. He was only satisfied when Derek Lipton finally pointed to the Vicar's hands.

"Take a look at them," he told the captain, "You don't get

hands like that from dipping babies into the christening font!"

Captain Coates looked and saw the scars and callouses on skin the texture of calf leather which would proclaim their bearer a man of the sea throughout his lifetime. Suddenly great doubt was replaced by an even greater mirth.

"You bastards!" shouted the captain, surveying the grinning brothers with a look of joyful incredulity. Then, in a much quieter though no less excited tone, he near whispered, "You've only gone and dumped a Vicar on me! Wait 'til news of this spreads around the ports, I can see free pints lined up for me from here to Fiddlers' Green. This is a tale I will have to tell over and over again."

And early the next morning, with none of the ceremony which accompanied her arrival, the *'Joan'* slipped her mooring lines and set her bows to the harbour entrance. The Pilot, who went on board to navigate the vessel until she was clear of the harbour's narrow channels, also supplied the hands who would work the ship for this critical part of the voyage. Once clear of these channels the Pilot and his crew were disembarked onto the Pilot Cutter: as this craft turned to head back into the harbour it would then be left to Captain Coates to sail his ship single-handedly until his own crew, each one of them unconscious below decks, regained their senses and discovered their new station in life. This process would take several hours, by which time the *'Joan'* would be well out of sight of land. Thus there was no option for the involuntary hands to do anything except bend to their work and hope for a speedy end to the voyage.

It was quite late in the afternoon when The Reverend Michael Grape opened his eyes and slowly took in his surroundings. He was still feeling groggy from the sleeping draught, which had been swiftly administered when he had started showing signs of recovering from the blow which he had received with the cosh. He could only, therefore, assimilate and deal with one piece of information at a time: I am on board a ship, he told himself. Then, holding on to that thought, he began struggling to work out why he was on a ship. To assist his thinking he closed his eyes: I am on board a ship because I am a sailor, I am in the Royal Navy, he told himself. But, no, he reminded himself, you left the Navy and became a Vicar. Or did I? If I had done that I would not be on board a ship now. He pondered on this for a while until a new thought suddenly struck him: he opened his eyes and looked around his accommodation. This, he told himself, is not a ship of the Royal Navy. It is filthy. He closed his eyes again and concentrated on recalling his recent past, searching for any clues which would explain why he was on board a ship. Being a one time man of the sea it did not take him long to realise what had befallen him: boarders! I was walking through the town and I was jumped upon by boarding masters. With this realisation came a certain contentment and The Reverend Michael Grape even allowed himself a small smile. It is alright, he reasoned, it has all been a terrible mistake. They did not know that he was the Vicar, they must have been waiting for somebody else, all he would now have to do is to explain the error to the captain of this ship and he would be returned to the town. Satisfied that he finally had a full grasp of the situation, the Vicar then set himself the task of trying to remember how to use his limbs - a skill which seemed to have temporarily deserted him. Twenty minutes later, having had some success in simple movements of his arms and legs, he felt confident enough to stand up and even to attempt walking. This operation, though not without a few minor mishaps, proved to be well within his capabilities. It was certainly sufficient for the task of seeking an audience with the captain who, he felt sure, would be most embarrassed when he learned of the dreadful error perpetrated by the boarders. But, he told himself, I must remember to move very slowly and very carefully.

So it was, slowly and carefully, that The Reverend Michael Grape made his way up to the main deck. Once at this destination, stood in the sunlight, a blast of fresh sea air, invigorating and clean, worked its magic upon his general state of well being: he took several deep breaths and felt his fuddled head clearing more and more with each one. He looked out across the swell of the sea and felt his life-long affinity with the oceans stir within him. Its magnetic pull held him transfixed and, for a brief moment, he was ready to forget his mission to God and embrace this life forever. Subconsciously he had adopted the stance of a sailor, legs apart and hands clasped behind his back. Standing thus he was able to feel the gentle roll of the vessel and to move with it: become at one with the surging green mass which stretched as far as the eye could see. This was his element, this is what he was born to, this was.....

"Good afternoon sir."

His train of thought abruptly broken by a voice behind him, the Vicar turned and found himself stood face-to-face with Captain Coates. In an instant The Reverend Michael Grape became once again a man of the cloth.

"Oh, er, good afternoon captain. Listen, there has been a dreadful mistake."

The Vicar then proceeded to explain who he was, how he had been erroneously taken by the boarders and why he had to be taken back to his flock. During this latter part he became highly animated, his speech littered with suitable quotes from the scriptures. This led him into talking about prawns, prawnmen and the 'Fishermens' Praying Rooms', which then gave rise to an even more urgent demand that the *'Joan'* should turn around and head back to port. Captain Coates listened patiently to this tirade and then, after raising his hat in a gesture of politeness, drove a powerful fist into the Vicar's face. Thus it was that, from a position sprawled upon the deck, The Reverend Michael Grape learned in very colourful language what duties were expected of him on board the *'Joan'*. It was also explained to him that should he forget any of these duties then the captain's fist was always there to remind him. Satisfied that this brief, but very intense, period of training would be sufficient, Captain Coates ended on a note of warning; "And if I catch you trying to organise the hands into Sunday prayers I'll want to know why you've got the energy. You are on board my ship to work and work you bloody well will, 'til you bloody well drop. You can make port or you can be shark food, it's up to you!"

And so work The Reverend Michael Grape did: but on his own terms. Once he had time to reflect upon, and accept, his change in circumstance he embraced them with the patience of Job. It was the Lord's wish that he should suffer the privations of life on board the *'Joan'*, it was all part of the Almighty's plan to rid the world of prawns. Thus reconciled, he set about proving to captain and crew alike that his disciplined approach to seamanship, forged within the Royal Navy, was of the highest standard. It has to be noted, however, that he completely failed to notice any correlation between the bullying tactics which he had used to fill his pews and those used to crew the *'Joan'*.

But the determination to transform the *'Joan'* into a clean well run vessel, with or without Captain Coates's leave, did not ever blind him to his real mission in life. When he did get the opportunity to cease in his labours for a few moments he would gaze over the stern of the ship. As he indulged in this moment of reverie he would think of the town, now many sea miles away, and murmur; "I will be back!"

The quiet determination with which he spoke these words was driven by the Prawning Admiral's one last salvo in the departing Vicar's direction. Once the Lipton Boys had dealt with their victim Master Miles gained access to the Vicarage: here he had gathered a few items of the Vicar's clothing to accompany the man on his voyage. Stuffing them into a kitbag he could not resist enclosing a note which contained nothing more than the lines of a local piece of doggerel;

> If the town was a fish pool,
> And the men of the town fish.....

~~*~~

> ...There'd be a pool f'r the Devil,
> An' fish f'r 'is dish!

Boathook Bald's recital caused his two drinking companions to cheer loudly and appreciatively. One of these fellow imbibers sharing a 'God–forgive-me' which stood on the table in front of them was Fiddler Crabbe: he had cheered because this doggerel was part of their town heritage and the working folk never tired of reciting it or hearing it. The second companion was the Visitor: he had cheered because he was drunk and happy, to the point where he felt like cheering at everything and nothing. He turned to face Boathook Bald and, smiling foolishly, asked him;

"What did writ?"

The two men, their heads swaying gently as if disturbed

by a light breeze, stared at each other for a few moments before both realised that the words had not made any sense. The Visitor decided he needed to make a second attempt at asking the question, only this time he would use words which, when strung together in the correct order, would form a coherent sentence. In this endeavour he was largely successful, certainly enough to make his meaning known;

"Who wrote it?" he wanted to know, "Was it you or someone not you?"

Before the prawnman could form a reply to this enquiry, Fiddler Crabbe took it upon himself to furnish the Visitor with the requested information.

"That's 'undreds o'years old that is," he declared, raising one hand in the air and using it to indicate a time long past, "They reckons that it's what the folks in the towns an' villages used t'say 'bout them that lived 'ere. They reckoned we was all rogues an' vill'ans an' things like that!"

He stood up and shouted at the towns and villages for miles around;

"An' we are, an' we always 'as been, an' we always will be!"

And then, satisfied that this message had carried to every corner of the county, he sat down to reacquaint himself with the giant cider pot.

It was the Visitor's final night in the town: the last week of his stay here having been in total contrast to the days following his arrival. When Boathook Bald had returned from his island hideaway following the sailing of the *'Joan'* it was to discover that, in a highly exuberant mood, the Prawning Masters had given their crews a week's holiday. It has to be noted, however, that this apparent gesture of largess was entirely due to the Masters themselves wishing to indulge in their own celebrations. Furthermore, it was by no means down to cynicism that more than one crewman was heard to mutter;

"If they be givin' us a week off now, you mark my words, we'll be payin' f'r it later on when they've all sobered up an' re'lised what they done!"

But to Boathook Bald the future was to come and now was now: he would make the most of a holiday, made more pleasant for him personally by the knowledge that he was not going to have to carry out his plan with regards to the Vicar and Miss Simpson – a plan which had seemed somewhat daunting once the effects of the cider had worn off. As his personal finances were pitifully low he was pleased to discover that the Visitor was still in town The prawnman wasted no time in seeking him out and making him aware that, during his time in hiding, he had thought of a lot more customs and traditions to relate. The Visitor, though not wishing to indulge in further research, was nevertheless quite content to fund the other's pleasure. Having never been one to socialise greatly in the past he was grateful to have a seasoned drinker as a companion: he foolishly believed that in such company he would have an ideal introduction to the gentle art of going out for a drink. For the first time in his life he walked into an ale house as a customer in his own right, his intention being to be guided by the actions of his fellow drinkers within. The Visitor was not to know that Paradise, the ale house in question, knew nothing of gentle arts: the subtle guidance which he had sought had become a baptism with fire - with a few fireworks thrown in for good measure.

In later years, when his mind drifted back to his week of holiday in the town, he would marvel at how he could harbour such fond memories about a period of which he could actually recall very little: it was one long drunken fog. Boathook Bald had introduced him to Fiddler Crabbe who in turn introduced him to Eli Silver. These three, sometimes all together and on other occasions any combination of them, were his drinking partners throughout the week: they were certainly qualified to steer him towards a less rigid view of the world than he had hitherto been used to. Eli Silver, a stocky character with a shock of long blond hair, professed himself to be 'A fisherman, a singer, a rigger and a singer. In that order!' before launching himself into a song. This air seemed to have a countless number of verses and concerned the exploits of an English sailor in a Man o'War during the Napoleonic age. Apart from a smattering of nautical phrases, it did seem to concentrate more on descriptions of the Jolly Jack Tar's various sexual activities than it did about shipboard life. The song was well received by the company in Paradise: each verse drew a round of applause and laughter and, by its climax, saw Fiddler Crabbe and Jane the Stain mimicking some of the actions related. Watching this outrageous pantomime the Visitor added a new word to his private lexicon: Fun. Another lifetime first for him, he was witnessing unbridled reckless fun and he was surprised at how easily this commodity could be obtained.

It was Eli who, in a quieter moment, had educated the Visitor in the matter of cider production.

"Y'won't taste cider like this," he nodded toward a freshly replenished 'God–forgive-me'. "not anywhere in the world. Ol' Leggy makes it 'imself an' 'e keeps the recipe a secret but there's one or two things 'bout it that 'e's proud of. Like what meat's been in it..."

"Meat?" interrupted the Visitor, "He makes cider from meat?"

"No, 'e makes it from apples, an' 'e won't tell any other bugger what varieties 'e uses," answered Eli. "but once the cider's fermentin' y'ave t'chuck a lump o'meat in, an' it's got t'be rottin' meat. Y'don't get the right flavour out of it otherwise."

If the Visitor felt a momentary pang of revulsion at this information it was soon overcome by a drunken logic within his brain. Whatever went into the cider, it reasoned, it tasted good, it had not poisoned him and, most importantly, Eli Silver (who was his new best friend) had said that it was right and proper and therefore it must be so.

"Now then," continued Eli, "Most o'your cider farms uses rats 'cos there's always plenty o'them 'round a cider press. Y'don't even 'ave to trap 'em 'cos the stupid little fuckers jus' fall in the vats anyway! But Leggy always 'ooks the rats out, 'e swears blind by a bit o'beef y'see. But the best stuff 'e makes is the late summer one, that's jus' pure nectar an' it's all down t'wasps!"

"Wasps?" was all that the enthralled audience needed to reply by way of encouragement.

"Yeah, wasps." Confirmed the informant who required little prompting, having by now warmed to his theme.

"Leggy reckons that it's an ol' fam'ly tradition an' it's what makes the cider so special. All the local kids knows they c'n earn a few shillin's by catchin' 'em f'r 'im - they got t'be live mind, if there's any squashed ones get in it c'n ruin the whole vat. So Leggy is mos' careful t'sort through 'em. 'e reckons on usin' two or three 'andfuls o'wasps per gallon."

Smacking his lips at the mere thought of this brew, Eli Silver sat back in his seat adopting the expression of one for whom life had been made complete. This repose, however, lasted not one minute for no devotee of Paradise would sit comfortable whilst still able to leap about. Of a sudden his voice, that same voice which spoke with that rare gentle melodic quality, the voice which could hold an audience with both speech and song, now turned into an almighty roar;

"Fiddler Crabbe, I need music!"

Grabbing the bodhran, an instrument that he was rarely seen without, Eli leapt to his feet and launched into a song amid cheers from the assembled imbibers. By the time the song had reached its second verse, Fiddler Crabbe was ready to join in and the two musicians were soon using their respective musical instruments to push each other along, a determined campaign by both parties to increase the tempo in order to test the other's ability to keep pace. Eventually Eli's vocal chords were unable to cope with the breakneck speed of the music and the pair then embarked upon a series of reels. At one with each other musically, Fiddler Crabbe's bow brought forth note perfect tunes whilst Eli Silver kept time with unerring sympathy. This was in contrast to the cacophony of sound created by their enthusiastic audience: fists and tankards were banged onto table tops, hands clapped, feet stamped and the frequent shriek would rent the air. It seemed as if the whole of Paradise had lost their sanity and were only aware of the music which held a spell over their limbs.

Yet there were three people in the room who did not move: One was mine host Dave Legg who stood behind the bar, ever alert for one of those collective mood swings amongst his clientele, the sudden change from an air of jollity to a full scale riot. Another was one of the whores, whose given name of Sylvia had been corrupted to 'Sin-bag' Along with her sisters-in-trade she had noticed the presence of a stranger in their midst, none other than the Visitor. Noting that he was not the usual type of customer attracted to Paradise they watched him, discussed him and divined that he was that rarity among the men that they generally had contact with: in short, a virgin. Not a puppy still wet behind the ears kind of a virgin but a full grown man for whom this pleasure had been elusive: to these ladies of the night this made him a trophy to be competed for, which they had done using a set of dice. Sin-bag had won and now she sat keeping a close eye upon her prize. She would not receive a single penny for lifting her skirt later but this was of no account: the whores saw these occasional diversions as an amusing relief to the grind of their nightly work.

The third person not moving to the music was the object of her vigil: the Visitor himself. Leaning against a wall he was, for the moment, content to stand, watch and smile. In truth he was incapable of doing much else, the alcohol that he was unused to making him feel suddenly dizzy. And it was at this point that he experienced an event which was to change his life forever, though he would never be able to fully explain what had taken place.

Though Paradise occupied no great floor space it was, during such wild sessions, not easy to see from one side of the room to the other: the candlelight, the smoke from the fire and a dozen or so briars, these elements were compounded by the dust raised as feet were stamped by the revellers. Added to this was the Visitor's cider fogged vision: a new experience for him and one which he was enjoying greatly. All that his brain could take in was the sensation of pleasure at seeing the sea of happy faces and, to top it all, he was one of them. Then, from the other side of the room, one face in particular stood out. With a sobering shock the Visitor realised that it was his father. The initial reaction to this was to turn away as he felt overcome by both guilt and confusion: the logical part of his brain was telling him that this could not be, his father was dead whilst the emotional part was saying that it was his father, Furthermore, he would not be best pleased to witness his son in this state of advanced inebriation.

Though he dreaded the paternal disproving gaze, the Visitor could not stop himself from taking another look across the room: as before, he saw his father looking at him intently. But there was no sternness in his eyes, there was love mixed with amusement. As their eyes locked for a moment the Visitor knew that his father was pleased to see him enjoying himself like this, the amused indulgence of a parent seeing their offspring join the world of adulthood for the first time. A second or two of this contact is all that the son was permitted before the vision was gone and, try as he might, the Visitor could see him no more. But that instant changed his life forever: he knew why his father had appeared to him, he was aware of his father's approval and encouragement. So little was said yet nothing was left unsaid, the son now knew he could feel truly part of his family's heritage: he would have no need to don his father's uniform again.

During this encounter the Visitor had momentarily lost all sense of his present surroundings: it was as if Paradise and its clamour had faded away. But it suddenly came back to him with a brutal harshness and once again he was caught up in its noise and bustle. He wanted to dance, to join in with the throng, but as he attempted to move in order to throw himself into the revelries he felt his legs give way beneath him. Slowly he started to slide down the wall. He could do nothing to halt this collapse and was resigned to it being total, once he could go no further, he reasoned, it would simply be a case of then having to stand up again: drunken logic making this course of action the easiest to follow. But the expected contact with the floor did not materialise, his progress downwards was halted by a pair of hands that came from nowhere and lifted him upright once more. He saw that his saviour was a woman who was now smiling kindly at him.

"I think you need to lie down." The woman took him firmly by the arm and guided him toward the door. "My name is Sylvia, I live nearby so we'll get you there and I'll soon have you feeling better. What is your name?"

"Thank you, yes, I do need a little rest." The Visitor responded gratefully to Sin-bag's encouraging tone, "My name is Philip."

Epilogue

It was the start of the Prawning Season and Master Miles, still buoyed up by the esteem of his peers for his handling of the lease, was in an exceptionally good mood. All was optimism as he made his way to the Fisherman's Dock: he felt it was going to be a profitable season. Earlier that day he had been to a sitting with an artist who lived in a nearby Victorian suburb of the town, his fellow Masters in the Prawning Fleet having commissioned a portrait of their Admiral which would take pride of place in The Club; an honour indeed! And from his place on board the Prawning Vessel *'Prudence'* Boathook Bald watched his Master's approach intently. From the Admiral's gait, and his hail-fellow-well-met greetings to all and sundry along his way, the crewman decided it would be a good day to ask something which had been much on his mind of late. His confidence for this was boosted by the unexpected greeting he received as the Master stepped on board.

"Good morning Boakhook."

"Good mornin' Master Miles," Boathook Bald looked sheepishly at the deck, "I were wond'rin' if I may ask y'somethin', beggin' y'pardon Master."

"Of course you can. Speak up."

"Well, y'see, it's like this......"

Being aware that his request would entail using far more than his weekly allowance of twenty-five words, the crewman paused at this point in order to jump over the side of the boat. It was from a position of treading water beside the vessel that he was able to continue speaking to the Master.

"....I was wantin' t'know, seein' 'as 'ow the d'vorce is far away now, if I c'n get married again?"

The Admiral of the Prawning Fleet looked at his crewman. What he saw was a pile of rags: dirty, smelly, but a very faithful and hardworking pile of rags nevertheless. All the man was asking for was the chance of a little happiness.

"No," he replied abruptly, "You can't. Now get on with your work!"